STAAR

STATE OF TEXAS ASSESSMENTS OF ACADEMIC READINESS

GRADE 5
SCIENCE

Jason Reed

First Edition

Table of Contents

Introduction

About the STAAR Science Tests

The 5th-grade Science STAAR test includes a total of 42 questions. Among these, there are multiple-choice questions where students must choose the correct answer from the provided options. The remaining questions are open-ended, requiring students to express their thoughts and provide explanations.

About the Science STAAR Full-Length Tests in This Book

The practice questions included in this book are designed to replicate the Science STAAR tests accurately. They provide your child with a valuable opportunity to understand key concepts and familiarize themselves with the format, types of questions, and time constraints they will encounter on the STAAR test.

The tests target all required categories, ensuring your child masters Matter and Energy, Force, Motion, and Energy, Earth and Space, and Organisms and Environments.

Repetition is a proven method for effective studying. We firmly believe in the power of practice, which is why we've included multiple practice questions for each STAAR category in this book.

By working through these practice tests, your child can:

- **Improve time management:** They will become adept at managing their time efficiently during the test, ensuring they complete all sections within the allocated time.

- **Build confidence:** Repeatedly solving problems in a format similar to the actual test will boost their confidence, reducing anxiety on test day.

- **Identify weaknesses:** These questions will help pinpoint and target specific areas where your child may need additional review and practice.

- **Enhance problem-solving skills:** Regular practice hones problem-solving skills and strategies, enabling your child to tackle challenging questions effectively.

- **Score higher:** Through focused practice and familiarization with the test structure, your child can strive for higher scores on the STAAR test.

The questions in this book closely mirror those found in the actual STAAR tests, ensuring that your child gains a deep understanding of the test's structure and content. By working through these practice questions, they will be well-equipped to achieve success on the Science STAAR test.

As parents, educators, or instructors, your support and encouragement play a pivotal role in your child's academic journey. We encourage you to actively engage with your child's science education, using these resources as tools to enhance their learning experience.

Dear Parents,

Thank you for purchasing the STAAR Science Practice Workbook for grade 5.

As an independent author, I have put a great deal of effort into ensuring the quality and accuracy of the content provided. Each problem has been carefully solved and reviewed to provide the best learning experience.

However, despite the rigorous efforts to maintain high standards, occasional mistakes can occur. If you come across any errors or discrepancies in the book or the solutions, please do not hesitate to reach out. Your feedback is invaluable in helping to improve the quality of this workbook.

For any corrections, questions, or comments, please contact me at *jasonreedbooks@gmail.com*. Your assistance in identifying and rectifying any issues is greatly appreciated.

Thank you for your understanding and support.

Sincerely,

Jason Reed

PRACTICE TEST 1

GET STARTED →

1.  The Earth moves around the Sun while continuously rotating on its axis. How much time does it take for the Earth to complete one full orbit around the Sun?

(A) 24 hours

(B) 30 days

(C) 6 months

(D) 1 year

2. Which planet in our solar system is closest to the Sun?

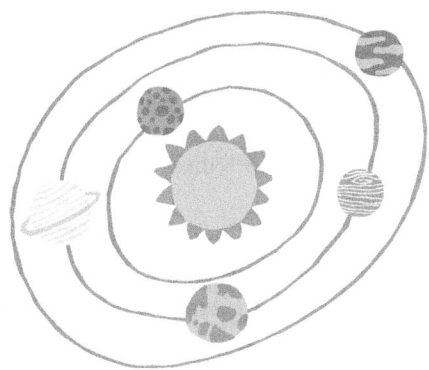

(A) Mercury

(B) Venus

(C) Earth

(D) Mars

3. What causes the phenomenon of day and night on Earth?

(A) The Earth's orbit around the Sun.

(B) The Earth's rotation on its axis.

(C) The tilt of the Earth's axis.

(D) The Earth's gravitational pull.

4. What is a food chain?

- (A) A type of plant structure in charge of nutrient and water distribution.
- (B) A chain used to catch food by different insect and arachnid species.
- (C) A series of organisms each dependent on the next as a source of food.
- (D) A sequence of weather events that influence the availability of food.

5. Which of the following food chains correctly shows the flow of energy in a marine ecosystem?

- (A) Plankton → fish → seals → sharks
- (B) Seals → sharks → fish → plankton
- (C) Fish → sharks → seals → plankton
- (D) Plankton → seals → sharks → fish

6. In a freshwater lake ecosystem, what is the primary source of energy?

- (A) Phytoplankton
- (B) Fish
- (C) Birds
- (D) Algae

7. How can we reduce our carbon footprint?

A By driving around your city to visit new restaurants.

B By taking note of all the types of waste you produce.

C By travelling to natural protected areas by airplane.

D By using public transport and reducing energy consumption.

8. Which inference can be made by comparing these diagrams?

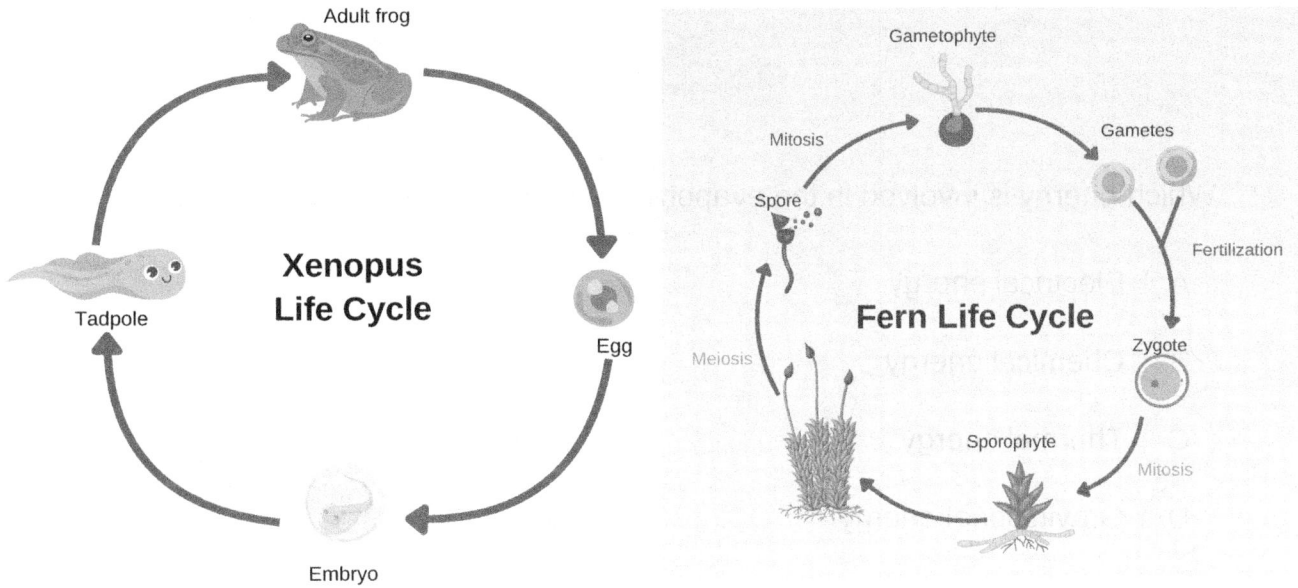

A Plants require more kinetic energy than animals to undergo changes from a young organism to a mature organism.

B Both animals and plants undergo a series of changes throughout their life cycle that enable them to survive and reproduce.

C Animals are more likely than plants to adapt to changes in the environment for survival.

D Animals and plants mutually depend on each other for survival.

7

9. A student observes the water cycle in the following image.

The Water Cycle

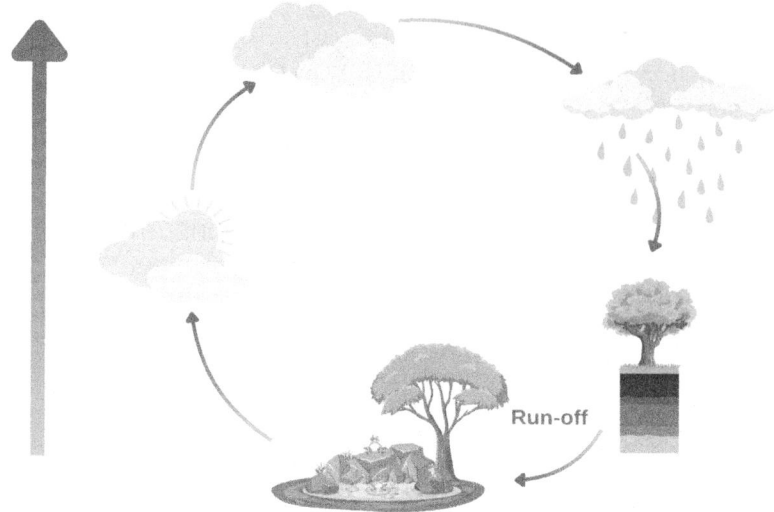

Run-off

Which energy is involved in the evaporation of water from lake to clouds?

A   Electrical energy

B   Chemical energy

C   Thermal energy

D   Gravitational energy

10. A student places a piece of iron in a fire. What causes the iron to become red-hot?

A   The iron absorbs heat from the fire.

B   The iron reflects heat from the fire.

C   The iron passes through the heat from the fire.

D   The iron emits heat to the fire.

11. This question has two parts. Answer Part A with the help of the following image. Then, answer Part B.

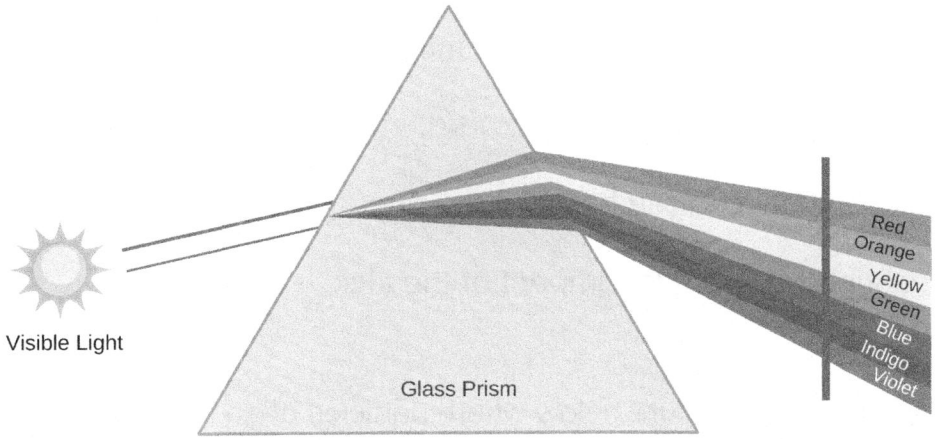

Part A

A student shines a beam of white light through a prism, and the light spreads out into a spectrum of colors. Which statement BEST describes what happens to the light as it passes through the prism?

A   The light is absorbed by the prism.

B   The light is reflected by the prism.

C   The light is refracted by the prism.

D   The light is diffused by the prism.

Part B

Which statement BEST explains the answer to Part A?

A   The prism absorbs different wavelengths of light at different rates.

B   The prism reflects different wavelengths of light at different angles.

C   The prism bends (refracts) different wavelengths of light in different amounts.

D   The prism diffuses the light, scattering it in all directions.

12. A soccer ball is kicked across a field. What force causes the ball to eventually stop rolling?

(A) Air resistance pushing against the ball.

(B) Gravity pulling the ball downward.

(C) Friction between the ball and the grass.

(D) Elastic force from the impact of the kick.

13. Students observe the picture below where particles of an unknown material are added to pure water. After mixing, the particles sediment to the bottom of the container.

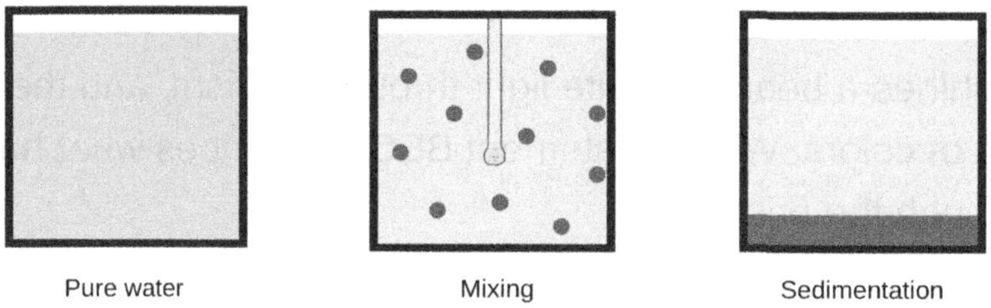

Pure water   Mixing   Sedimentation

Which conclusion can be made from image?

(A) The particles have a higher density than water.

(B) The particles have a lower density than water.

(C) The particles have the same density as water.

(D) The particles dissolve completely in water.

14. A laser pointer is directed at a mirror on a wall. The beam reflects off the mirror and hits another wall. What property of light does this demonstration show?

(A) Light absorption

(B) Light reflection

(C) Light diffusion

(D) Light refraction

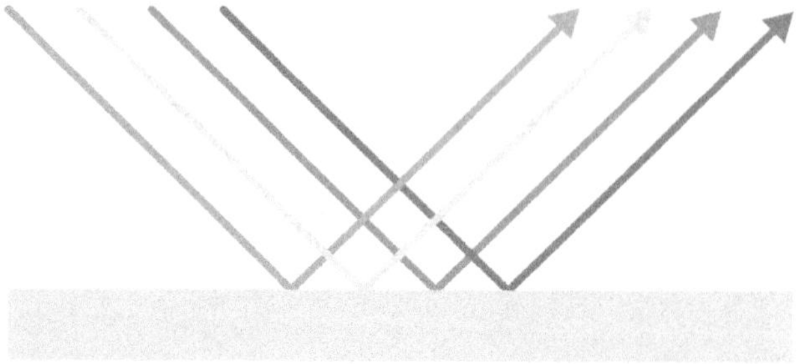

15. What process causes dew to form on grass in the morning?

A   Water vapor melted on the grass.

B   Water vapor evaporated off the grass.

C   Water vapor condensed on the grass .

D   Water vapor froze on the grass.

16. A student has a mixture of iron nails, marbles, and sand. How can the student separate the nails from the mixture?

A   Dissolve the mixture in water and then filter it.

B   Use a magnet to attract the nails.

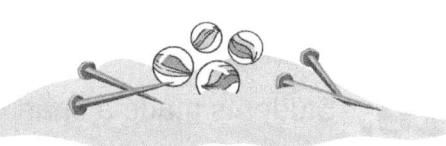

C   Pour the mixture through filter paper.

D   Heat the mixture to melt the iron nails.

17. In a kitchen experiment, a student mixes cooking oil and vinegar. How can the student separate the oil from the vinegar?

A   Heat the mixture until the oil evaporates.

B   Use a magnet to attract the oil droplets.

C   Pour the mixture through filter paper.

D   Place the mixture in a refrigerator to solidify the oil.

18. A table of the properties of four different samples of matter is shown.

Sample	Conducts Electricity	Conducts Heat	Soluble in Water	Physical State at Room Temperature
1	No	No	No	Solid
2	Yes	Yes	No	Solid
3	No	Yes	Yes	Liquid
4	Yes	Yes	No	Liquid

Which answer is correct for sample 1?

A) Sample 1 is plastic.

B) Sample 1 is iron.

C) Sample 1 is alcohol.

D) Sample 1 is oxygen.

19. Students made a chart classifying animal behaviors.

Inherited	Learned
Turtle nesting on a beach	Bee building a hive
Chick imprinting on its mother	Dolphin learning tricks in captivity
Caterpillar spinning a coccon	Monkey washing food before eating

Which animal behavior is NOT correctly classified?

A) Turtle nesting on a beach.

B) Chick imprinting on its mother.

C) Caterpillar spinning a cocoon.

D) Bee building a hive.

20. Volcanoes and calderas are two geological features found in volcanic regions. Which statement best describes how volcanoes and calderas are similar?

- (A) Both are formed by underground magma chambers.
- (B) Both are created by erosion and weathering.
- (C) Both are part of tectonic plate boundaries.
- (D) Both are shaped by meteorite impacts.

21. This question has two parts. First, answer Part A. Then, answer Part B.

Part A

A student places an ice cube on a plate and leaves it at room temperature. Which statement BEST describes what will happen to the ice cube over time?

- (A) The ice cube will increase in size.
- (B) The ice cube will decrease in size.
- (C) The ice cube will remain the same size.
- (D) The ice cube will become warmer but remain solid.

Part B

Which statement BEST explains the answer to Part A?

- (A) The ice cube absorbs heat from the surroundings, causing it to melt.
- (B) The ice cube absorbs cold from the surroundings, causing it to grow.
- (C) The ice cube releases cold to the surroundings, causing it to stay solid.
- (D) The ice cube releases heat to the surroundings, causing it to remain the same size.

22. A student mixed salt into a glass of water and stirred it. After a few minutes, the salt particles were no longer visible, and the water tasted salty. What most likely happened to the salt?

(A) The salt evaporated into the air.

(B) The salt dissolved in the water.

(C) The salt sank to the bottom of the glass.

(D) The salt reacted with the water to form a new substance.

23. Which statement describes an animal interacting with a non-living part of the environment?

(A) A fish swims through water.

(B) A bird builds a nest in a tree.

(C) A cat chases a mouse.

(D) A cow eats grass.

24. A student drew the following pictures to show the day-night cycle of Earth.

Based on the pictures, how many hours of the nighttime is in a day-night cycle?

(A) 9 hours

(B) 10 hours

(C) 11 hours

(D) 24 hours

Sunrise: 7:15 AM
Sunset: 8:15 PM

14

25. Maple trees grow to be 10 to 45 meters tall. Their wide branches are covered with broad leaves, and their roots penetrate deeply into the soil. Maple trees drop their leaves in autumn.

Characteristics of Four Ecosystems

Ecosystem	Temperature	Yearly Precipitation	Soil
1	Cold winters and warm summers	Between 70 and 150 cm of rain	Moist, fertile soil
2	Warm year-round	Less than 40 cm of rain	Dry, sandy soil
3	Hot summers and mild winters	Between 60 and 100 cm of rain	Rocky, thin soil
4	Cool-to-cold winters and warm summers	More than 200 cm of rain	Well-drained, rich soil

In which ecosystem would forests of maple trees be most likely to survive?

(A) Ecosystem 1

(B) Ecosystem 2

(C) Ecosystem 3

(D) Ecosystem 4

26. A three-step process is shown: **Melting → Cooling → Crystallization**

Which of these are most likely formed by the process shown?

(A) Glaciers

(B) Igneous rocks

(C) Fossil fuels

(D) Sand dunes

27. Which material is known for being lightweight yet strong, and often used in airplane construction?

(A) Iron

(B) Aluminum

(C) Copper

(D) Lead

15

28. Which environmental impact is the most likely to occur when constructing a new dam in a river ecosystem?

- A) Increased habitats for fish species.

- B) Reduced water flow downstream.

- C) Improved air quality in the surrounding area.

- D) Decreased soil erosion in the region.

29. Students record characteristics of a bean plant. One student's list is shown.

Bean Plant Characteristics

- Thin, climbing stems with small leaves
- Roots growing deep into the soil
- White flowers
- Ten large green beans
- Six small green beans

Which bean plant characteristic is least likely to be inherited?

- A) Flower color

- B) Leaf shape

- C) Type of roots

- D) Number of beans

30. In which scenarios is light likely to undergo refraction? Select TWO correct answers.

- A) A student sees their reflection in a car window.

- B) Light reflects off a mirror onto a wall.

- C) A student watches a shadow move across a wall.

- D) Light bends when passing through a glass of water.

- E) A student observes stars through a telescope lens.

31. Why does the appearance of constellations change throughout the year?

(A) Earth revolves around the Sun.

(B) Earth rotates on its axis.

(C) The Sun revolves around Earth.

(D) Constellations rotate on their axes.

32. A student is learning about the inner and outer planets of our solar system. Which statements about the inner and outer planets are correct? Select TWO correct answers.

(A) Inner planets are closer to the Sun than outer planets.

(B) Outer planets are smaller and rockier than inner planets.

(C) Inner planets have fewer moons than outer planets.

(D) Outer planets have no atmospheres.

(E) Inner and outer planets are made of the same materials.

33. Which statement best explains why we have seasons on Earth?

(A) The Earth's distance from the Sun changes.

(B) The Earth rotates on its axis.

(C) The Earth's axis is tilted as it revolves around the Sun.

(D) The Sun's energy output varies throughout the year.

34. Which statement explains why we see different constellations at different times of the year?

    (A) The stars in the constellations are moving.

    (B) Earth's orbit around the Sun changes our view of the stars.

    (C) The Sun's light changes the visibility of stars.

    (D) Constellations move along with the moon.

35. A student learns that Earth has layers. Which of the following correctly lists these layers from the outermost to the innermost?

    (A) Crust, mantle, outer core, inner core.

    (B) Mantle, crust, inner core, outer core.

    (C) Crust, outer core, mantle, inner core.

    (D) Inner core, outer core, mantle, crust.

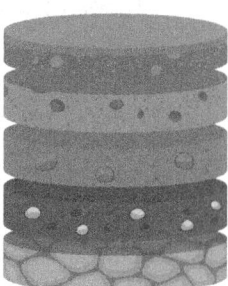

36. A picture and a description of a wolf and a polar seal are shown in the chart.

• Lives in forests, grasslands, and tundra across North America, Europe, and Asia.
• Its diet includes a variety of animals such as deer, elk, moose, and smaller mammals like rabbits and rodents.
• Wolves hunt in packs, using teamwork to catch their prey.
• They typically produce 4-6 offspring per year, and the offspring stay with the pack for several years.
• There are thousands of wolves in the wild, and they are not considered endangered.

• Lives in the icy waters and on the ice floes of the Arctic.
• Its diet consists mainly of fish, squid, and other marine organisms.
• Polar seals are excellent swimmers and can hold their breath for long periods to dive for food.
• They usually produce 1 offspring every year, and the offspring stay with their mother for about a year.
• Some estimates show that there are only a few hundred thousand polar seals left in the wild, making them vulnerable to environmental changes and hunting.

What are TWO likely reasons why wolves have a much greater population in the wild than polar seals?

(A) Wolves live in a wider range of habitats, including forests, grasslands, and tundra, while polar seals are limited to the Arctic region.

(B) Wolves produce fewer offspring, which means they need less food to sustain their population compared to polar seals.

(C) Wolves have a varied diet that includes many types of animals, while polar seals primarily eat fish and marine organisms, which may be affected by changes in the Arctic ecosystem.

(D) Polar seals are better swimmers, which helps them escape predators more effectively than wolves can.

(E) Wolves are more affected by environmental changes compared to polar seals, whose habitat is impacted by climate change.

37. Lions are apex predators that live in savannah ecosystems. They hunt large herbivores such as zebras and wildebeests. If lions are removed from savannah ecosystems, it can affect the savannah's communities. Which statement BEST predicts the effect of removing lions from savannah ecosystems?

(A) The variety of different organisms throughout savannah ecosystems will increase.

(B) Organisms that compete with the lions for food will decrease in numbers.

(C) Organisms that the lions prey on will increase in numbers.

(D) The savannah ecosystem will become a desert.

38. A group of animals is shown.

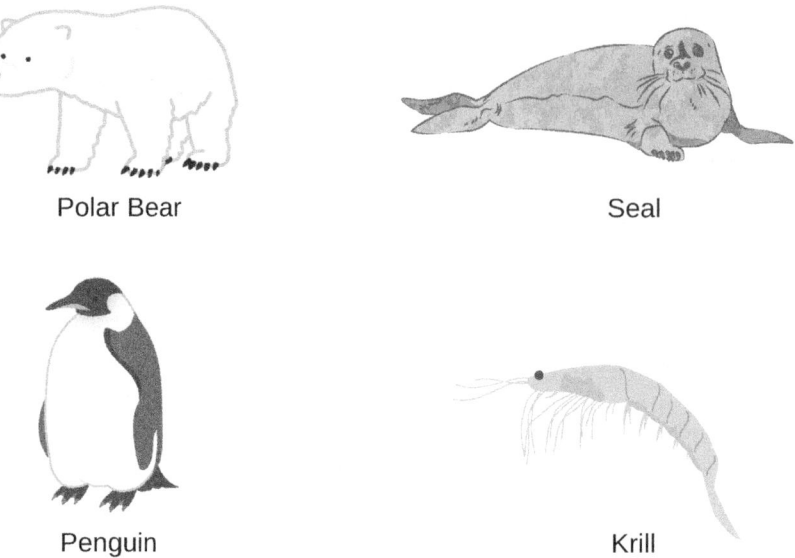

Polar Bear

Seal

Penguin

Krill

Which habitat are these animals BEST suited for?

- (A) A hot desert with sand dunes and cacti.
- (B) A tropical rainforest with dense foliage and high humidity.
- (C) An icy Arctic region with sea ice and cold temperatures.
- (D) A shallow coastal bay with sandy beaches and mangroves.

39. A student is pushing a heavy box across a smooth floor. What change will reduce the amount of force needed to move the box?

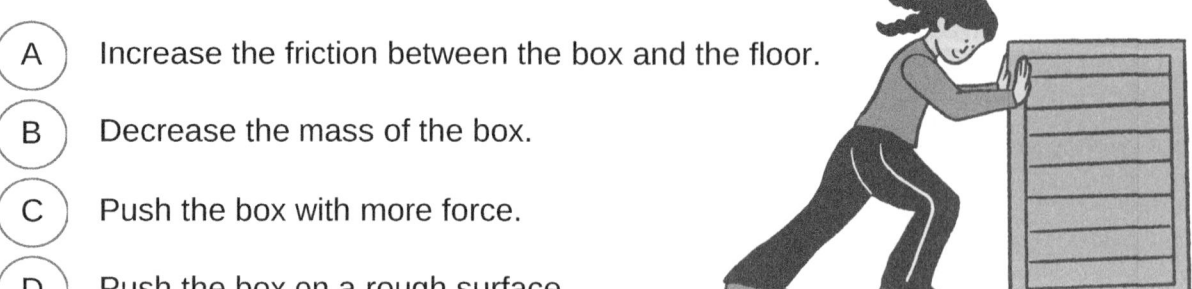

- (A) Increase the friction between the box and the floor.
- (B) Decrease the mass of the box.
- (C) Push the box with more force.
- (D) Push the box on a rough surface.

40. Which of these is an example of potential energy?

(A) A moving car

(B) A stretched rubber band

(C) A running horse

(D) A spinning top

41. Students want to determine how the type of ball affects the distance it rolls on a smooth surface. Which procedure should they follow for their experiment?

(A) Measure the distance rolled by different balls on different surfaces. Conduct three trials for each ball.

(B) Measure the distance rolled by the same ball on different surfaces. Conduct three trials for each surface.

(C) Measure the distance rolled by different balls on the same surface. Conduct three trials for each ball.

(D) Measure the distance rolled by the same ball on the same surface by different students. Conduct three trials for each student.

42. The circuit has five lightbulbs and four switches. If Switch 3 and 4 are closed, which lightbulbs will glow? Write the answer on the line provided. If none of the lightbulbs will glow, write NONE on the line: _____

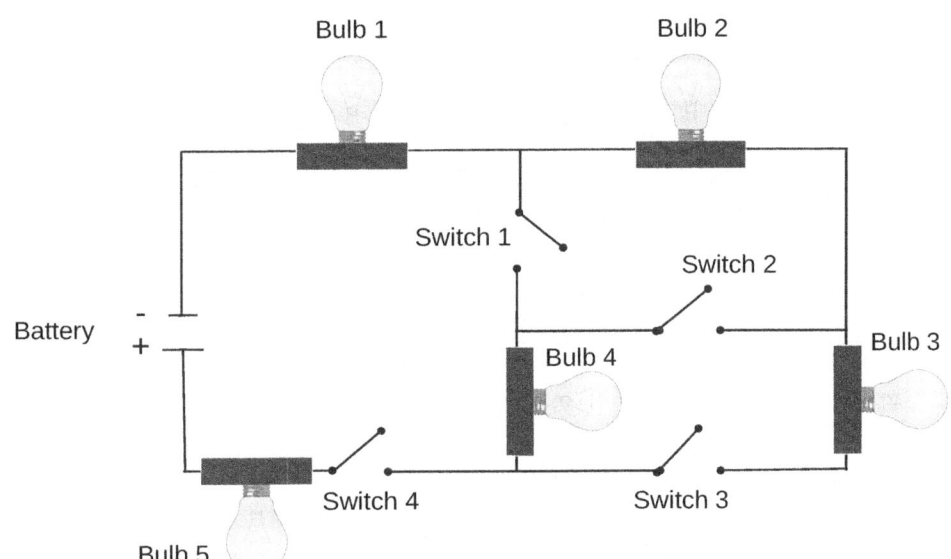

43. A baseball thrown through the air eventually falls back to the ground. What force causes the baseball to fall?

- (A) Wind resistance pushing against the baseball.

- (B) Gravity pulling the baseball downward.

- (C) Friction between the baseball and the air.

- (D) Elastic force from the impact of throwing the baseball.

44. A toy car rolls down a ramp and hits a stack of blocks, causing the blocks to scatter. What force caused the blocks to move?

- (A) Wind pushing against the blocks.

- (B) Gravity pulling the blocks downward.

- (C) Friction between the toy car and the ramp.

- (D) Elastic force from the impact of the toy car.

Answers Practice Test 1

1. D. 1 year
2. A. Mercury
3. B. The Earth's rotation on its axis
4. A. Plankton → fish → seals → sharks
5. C. A series of organisms each dependent on the next as a source of food.
6. A. Phytoplankton
7. D. By using public transport and reducing energy consumption.
8. B. Both animals and plants undergo a series of changes throughout their life cycle that enable them to survive and reproduce.
9. C. Thermal energy
10. A. The iron absorbs heat from the fire.
11. C. The light is refracted by the prism.
    C. The prism bends (refracts) different wavelengths of light in different amounts.
12. C. Friction between the ball and the grass
13. A. The particles have a higher density than water.
14. B. Light reflection
15. C. Water vapor condensed on the grass.
16. B. Use a magnet to attract the nails.
17. D. Place the mixture in a refrigerator to solidify the oil.
18. A. Sample 1 is plastic.
19. D. Bee building a hive.
20. A. Both are formed by underground magma chambers.
21. B. The ice cube will decrease in size.
A. The ice cube absorbs heat from the surroundings, causing it to melt.
22. B. The salt dissolved in the water.
23. A. A fish swims through water.
24. C. 11 hours
25. A. Ecosystem 1
26. B. Igneous rocks
27. B. Aluminum

28. B. Reduced water flow downstream.
29. D. Number of beans
30. D. Light bends when passing through a glass of water.
E. A student observes stars through a telescope lens.
31. A. Earth revolves around the sun.
32. A. Inner planets are closer to the sun than outer planets,
    C. Inner planets have fewer moons than outer planets.
33. C. The Earth's axis is tilted as it revolves around the sun.
34. B. Earth's orbit around the sun changes our view of the stars.
35. A. Crust, mantle, outer core, inner core
36. A. Wolves live in a wider range of habitats, including forests, grasslands, and tundra, while polar seals are limited to the Arctic region.
    C. Wolves have a varied diet that includes many types of animals, while polar seals primarily eat fish and marine organisms, which may be affected by changes in the Arctic ecosystem.
37. C. Organisms that the lions prey on will increase in numbers.
38. C. An icy Arctic region with sea ice and cold temperatures.
39. B. Decrease the mass of the box
40. B. A stretched rubber band
41. C. Measure the distance rolled by different balls on the same surface. Conduct three trials for each ball.
42. Bulbs 1, 2, 3, and 5.
43. B. Gravity pulling the baseball downward.
44. D. Elastic force from the impact of the toy car.

PRACTICE TEST 2

GET STARTED →

1. How long does it take for the Earth to complete one full rotation on its axis?

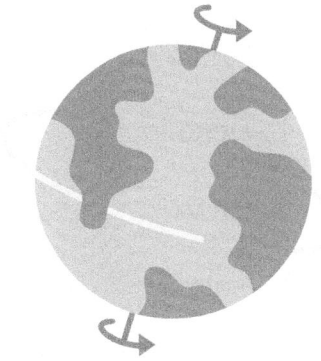

- (A) 24 hours
- (B) 30 days
- (C) 6 months
- (D) 1 year

2. How many planets in the solar system have rings?

- (A) One
- (B) Two
- (C) Three
- (D) Four

3. Which process describes the water cycle on Earth?

- (A) Photosynthesis
- (B) Plate tectonics
- (C) Evaporation, condensation, and precipitation
- (D) Erosion and sedimentation

4. Which food chain accurately represents a pond ecosystem?

- (A) Algae → insects → fish → turtles
- (B) Turtles → fish → insects → algae
- (C) Fish → turtles → algae → insects
- (D) Algae → turtles → fish → insects

25

5. Which of the following animals is a mammal?

A) Crocodile

B) Dolphin

C) Hawk

D) Salmon

6. This question has two parts. First, answer Part A. Then, answer Part B.

Part A
A student plants two identical seeds in separate pots. One pot is placed in a sunny window, and the other pot is placed in a dark closet. After a week, the seed in the sunny window has sprouted, but the seed in the closet has not. Which statement BEST explains why the seed in the sunny window sprouted faster?

A) The sunny window provides more water to the seed.

B) The sunny window has warmer temperatures, which help the seed grow.

C) The sunny window protects the seed from insects and pests.

D) The sunny window has more nutrients in the soil.

Part B
Which statement BEST explains the answer to Part A?

A) Seeds need sunlight to make their food through photosynthesis.

B) Seeds need darkness to absorb water and grow roots.

C) Seeds need heat to store energy for growth.

D) Seeds need nutrients from the soil to sprout roots.

26

7. What process do plants use to convert sunlight into chemical energy as illustrated at the image below?

(A) Transpiration

(B) Photosynthesis

(C) Erosion

(D) Germination

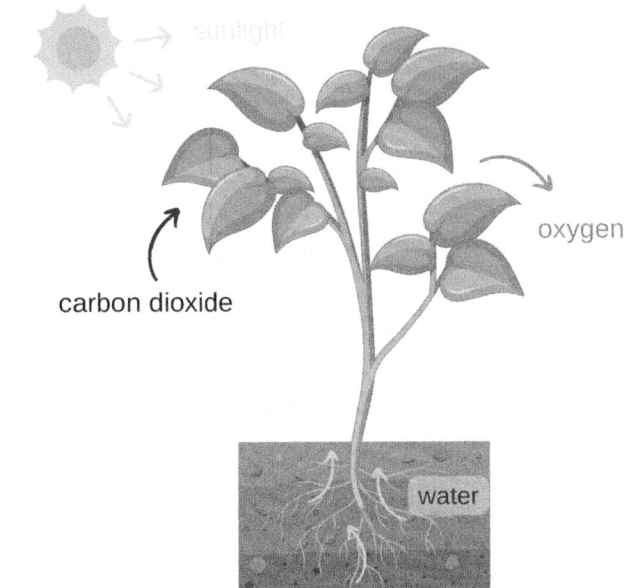

sunlight

oxygen

carbon dioxide

water

8. Students observe the diagram below showing the life cycle of silkworms. What do silkworms spin to create their cocoons?

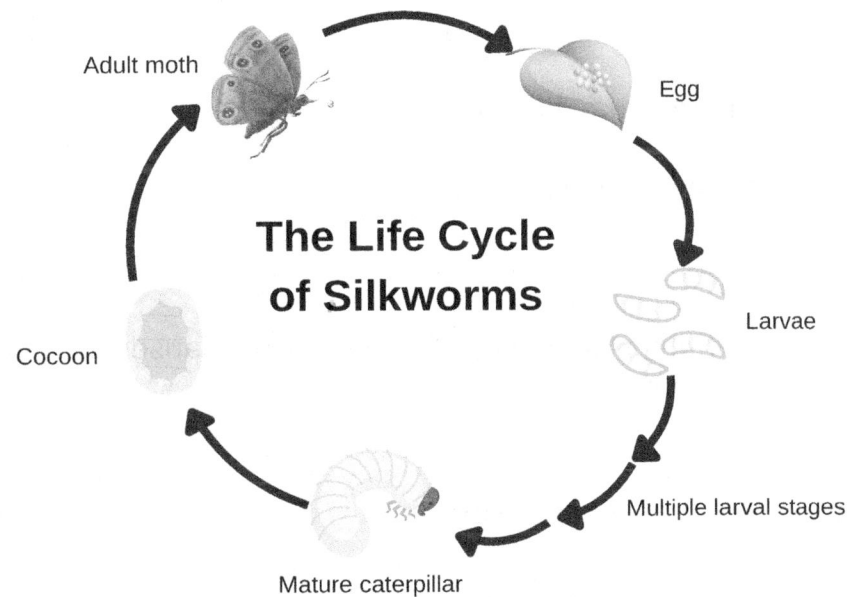

The Life Cycle of Silkworms

Adult moth

Egg

Larvae

Cocoon

Multiple larval stages

Mature caterpillar

(A) Silk thread

(B) Wax

(C) Cotton

(D) Wool

27

9. A student observed the time it took for a wet towel to dry after being hung outside on a clothesline. Which kind of energy primarily causes the water in the towel to evaporate?

A) Electrical energy from nearby power lines.

B) Chemical energy from the air.

C) Thermal energy from the sun.

D) Gravitational energy from the Earth.

10. A student places a metal spoon in a cup of hot soup. Which type of energy causes the spoon to become warm?

A) Mechanical energy from stirring.

B) Electrical energy from the microwave.

C) Chemical energy from the soup.

D) Thermal energy from the hot soup.

11. During a thunderstorm, a student sees lightning. What causes the thunderclap that follows shortly afterward?

A) Lightning absorbs heat from the air.

B) Lightning reflects sound waves.

C) Lightning generates sound waves.

D) Lighting creates a vacuum.

12. Which of the following is an example of kinetic energy?

A A book sitting on a shelf

B A stretched bowstring

C A moving car

D A compressed spring

13. Students observe the picture below where two different liquids are poured into a test tube, forming two phases.

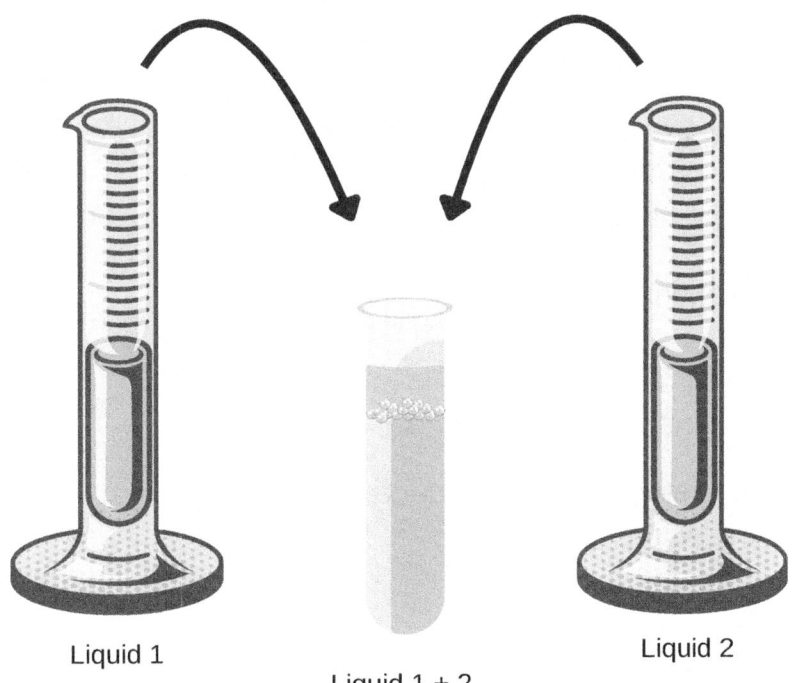

Liquid 1

Liquid 2

Liquid 1 + 2

Which conclusion can be made from image?

A Liquid 1 has a lower density than liquid 2.

B Liquid 2 has a lower density than liquid 1.

C Liquid 1 and 2 have the same density.

D Liquid 1 is soluble in liquid 2.

14. A helium-filled balloon is released and begins to rise. What force primarily causes the balloon to eventually come back down to the ground?

- (A) Air pressure from the surrounding atmosphere.
- (B) Gravity pulling the balloon downward.
- (C) Electrostatic force attracting the balloon to the ground.
- (D) Force from the helium inside the balloon.

15. What happens when the north poles of two magnets are brought close together?

- (A) They attract each other.
- (B) They repel each other.
- (C) They become neutral.
- (D) Nothing happens.

16. In an experiment, a student mixes sugar and water. How can the student separate the sugar from the water?

- (A) Use a magnet to attract the sugar particles.
- (B) Heat the mixture until the sugar crystallizes.
- (C) Pour the mixture through filter paper.
- (D) Allow the water to evaporate, leaving behind the sugar.

17. A student accidentally spills a mixture of ink and water. How can the student separate the ink from the water?

(A) Dissolve the mixture in more water and then filter it.

(B) Use a magnet to attract the ink particles.

(C) Pour the mixture through filter paper.

(D) Allow the water to evaporate, leaving behind the ink.

18. A table of the properties of four different samples of matter is shown.

Sample	Conducts Electricity	Conducts Heat	Soluble in Water	Physical State at Room Temperature
1	No	No	No	Solid
2	Yes	Yes	No	Solid
3	No	Yes	Yes	Liquid
4	Yes	Yes	No	Liquid

Which answer is correct for sample 2?

(A) Sample 2 is plastic.

(B) Sample 2 is iron.

(C) Sample 2 is alcohol.

(D) Sample 2 is oxygen.

19. How can fossils help scientists understand past climates?

(A) By showing weather patterns directly.

(B) By indicating the presence of ancient humans.

(C) By revealing what kinds of plants and animals lived in an area.

(D) By containing water samples from the past.

20. Caves and sinkholes are geological formations commonly found in karst landscapes. Which statement best describes how caves and sinkholes are similar?

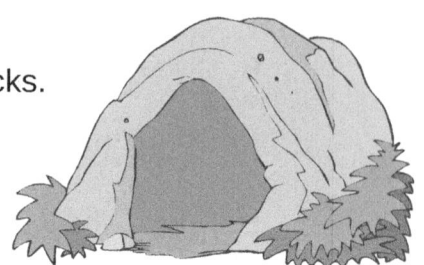

(A) Both are formed by volcanic activity.

(B) Both are created by deposition of sedimentary rocks.

(C) Both are carved out by chemical weathering.

(D) Both are results of glacier movements.

21. In our solar system, what is the order of the planets from the sun?

(A) Earth is the first planet, and Mars is the second.

(B) Mercury is the first planet, and Venus is the second.

(C) Mars is the first planet, and Jupiter is the second.

(D) Jupiter is the first planet, and Saturn is the second.

22. A student dropped a drop of ink into a glass of water and observed that the ink spread throughout the water, turning it blue. What most likely happened to the ink?

(A) The ink evaporated into the air.

(B) The ink dissolved in the water.

(C) The ink sank to the bottom of the glass.

(D) The ink froze in the cold water.

23. Imagine you are studying a species of mammals that live in cold Arctic regions. You observe the following characteristics:

- Thick fur coat
- A layer of blubber under the skin
- Small, rounded ears
- Large, padded paws
- Diet primarily consists of seals and fish

Based on these characteristics, which habitat do you think this mammal is most likely adapted to live in?

(A) Rainforest

(B) Arctic Tundra

(C) Desert

(D) Grassland

24. Why are the days longer during the summer compared to winter?

(A) The Earth moves closer to the Sun during the summer.

(B) The Earth tilts on its axis, causing more direct sunlight in one hemisphere.

(C) The Sun becomes larger in the sky during the summer.

(D) The Earth rotates more slowly during the summer.

25. Silkworms are known for their ability to produce silk used in textiles. Which habitat below would be most suitable for silkworms to thrive?

(A) Temperate forests with moderate rainfall and rich soil.

(B) Hot deserts with sandy and dry soil.

(C) Tropical rainforests with high humidity and abundant vegetation.

(D) Polar regions with icy conditions and sparse vegetation.

26. A three-step process is shown:

Evaporation → Condensation → Precipitation

Which of these are most likely formed by the process shown?

(A) Clouds

(B) Earthquakes

(C) Volcanoes

(D) Sedimentary rocks

27. A group of students is given four small blocks of the same size and instructed to place them in a tank of liquid. One block floats to the surface of the liquid. Two of the blocks float in the middle of the tank under the surface of the liquid. The last block sinks to the bottom of the tank.

Which conclusion is best supported by what the students observed?

(A) Two of the four blocks are soluble in the liquid

(B) All four blocks have different weights

(C) Each block is made of a different type of wood

(D) One of the blocks is less dense than the other three.

28. Which consequence would most likely result from the construction of a new airport in a rural area?

(A) Increased green space for wildlife.

(B) Decreased levels of noise pollution.

(C) Disruption of local wildlife habitats.

(D) Enhanced air quality in the region.

29. Students observe different types of vegetables in a garden. They focus on carrots and record their characteristics:

Carrot Characteristics:
- Edible taproot with orange color.
- Feathery leaves growing from the stem.
- Roots extending deep into the soil.
- Biennial plant with flowers in the second year.
- Grows best in loose, sandy soil.

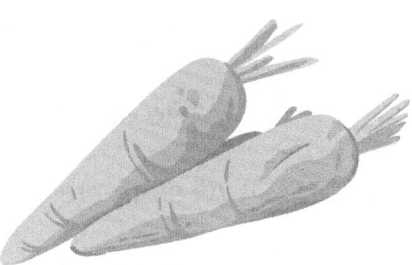

Which TWO characteristics of carrots are most likely inherited?

- (A) Root depth
- (B) Leaf shape
- (C) Flowering habit
- (D) Root color

30. Which activities involve light being refracted?

- (A) A student looks at a digital clock.
- (B) Light passes through a magnifying glass.
- (C) A student watches clouds drift across the sky.
- (D) A student sees their shadow on a sunny day.

31. What is the reason for the changing length of daylight hours throughout the year?

- (A) Earth revolves around the sun.
- (B) Earth rotates on its axis.
- (C) The sun revolves around Earth.
- (D) Daylight hours are constant throughout the year.

32. A student is comparing the features of different types of stars. Which statements about stars are correct? Select TWO correct answers.

(A) Red giants are larger than white dwarfs.

(B) White dwarfs are hotter than red giants.

(C) All stars are the same size.

(D) Stars do not produce light or heat.

(E) Stars are made of solid materials like planets.

33. Why do stars appear to twinkle when we look at them from Earth?

(A) Stars are constantly changing in brightness.

(B) Earth's atmosphere distorts the light from stars.

(C) Stars move quickly in space.

(D) The sun's light interferes with starlight.

34. A student looks at the night sky and sees the Milky Way. What is the Milky Way?

(A) A galaxy that includes our solar system.

(B) A star close to Earth.

(C) A constellation that appears in winter.

(D) A meteor shower that happens annually.

35. Which statement best describes why the Earth is habitable for humans?

- (A) Earth is the closest planet to the sun.

- (B) Earth has a thick atmosphere with oxygen.

- (C) Earth rotates once every 24 hours.

- (D) Earth has large polar ice caps.

36. A picture and a description of a mouse and a squirrel are shown in the chart.

• Lives in diverse habitats including forests, grasslands, agricultural areas, and urban settings worldwide. • Its diet consists of seeds, grains, fruits, and insects. • Mice are small and can hide in small spaces to escape predators. • They typically produce multiple litters per year, each containing 5-10 offspring. • Mice are very common and have large populations in the wild.	• Lives in forests, parks, and urban areas with trees worldwide. • Its diet primarily includes nuts, seeds, fruits, and occasionally insects. • Squirrels are agile climbers and can leap between branches to escape predators. • They typically produce 1-2 litters per year, each containing 2-8 offspring. • Squirrels are common, but their populations can be affected by habitat destruction and food availability.

What are TWO likely reasons why mice have a much greater population in the wild than squirrels?

- (A) Mice live in a wider range of habitats, including forests, grasslands, agricultural areas, and urban settings, while squirrels are primarily found in areas with trees.

- (B) Mice produce fewer offspring per year compared to squirrels, which means they need less food to sustain their population.

- (C) Mice have a more diverse diet that includes seeds, grains, fruits, and insects, while squirrels primarily eat nuts, seeds, and fruits.

- (D) Squirrels are agile climbers, which helps them escape predators more effectively than mice can.

- (E) Mice are significantly larger than squirrels, allowing them to dominate their habitats.

37. What is the main function of the leaves on a plant?

A. To absorb water

B. To produce seeds

C. To capture sunlight for photosynthesis

D. To anchor the plant

38. A group of animals is shown.

Trout

Heron

Beaver

Which habitat are these animals BEST suited for?

A. A deep-sea trench with low temperatures and high pressure.

B. A fast-flowing river with rocky rapids and waterfalls.

C. A deciduous forest with rich soil and four distinct seasons.

D. A coastal mangrove forest with brackish water and tangled roots.

39. Students are experimenting with pulling a wagon up a hill. What change will reduce the force needed to pull the wagon up the hill?

A. Increase the weight of the wagon.

B. Decrease the steepness of the hill.

C. Pull the wagon faster.

D. Use a shorter rope.

40. Which type of energy does a flashlight use to make light?

- (A) Kinetic energy
- (B) Solar energy
- (C) Electrical energy
- (D) Chemical energy

41. What type of energy does a windmill convert into electrical energy?

- (A) Kinetic energy
- (B) Thermal energy
- (C) Potential energy
- (D) Mechanical energy

42. When you rub your hands together on a cold day, what type of energy is produced, warming up your hands?

- (A) Electrical energy
- (B) Solar energy
- (C) Mechanical energy
- (D) Chemical energy

43. Students are testing how the size of a parachute affects the speed it falls from a height. Which procedure should they follow for their experiment?

- **A** Measure the speed of descent for parachutes of different sizes. Conduct three trials for each parachute.

- **B** Measure the speed of descent for the same parachute from different heights. Conduct three trials for each height.

- **C** Measure the speed of descent for parachutes of different sizes on different days. Conduct three trials for each size.

- **D** Measure the speed of descent for the same parachute from the same height by different students. Conduct three trials for each student.

44. The circuit has five lightbulbs and four switches. If Switch 2 and 3 are closed, which lightbulbs will glow? Write the answer on the line provided. If none of the lightbulbs will glow, write NONE on the line: _____

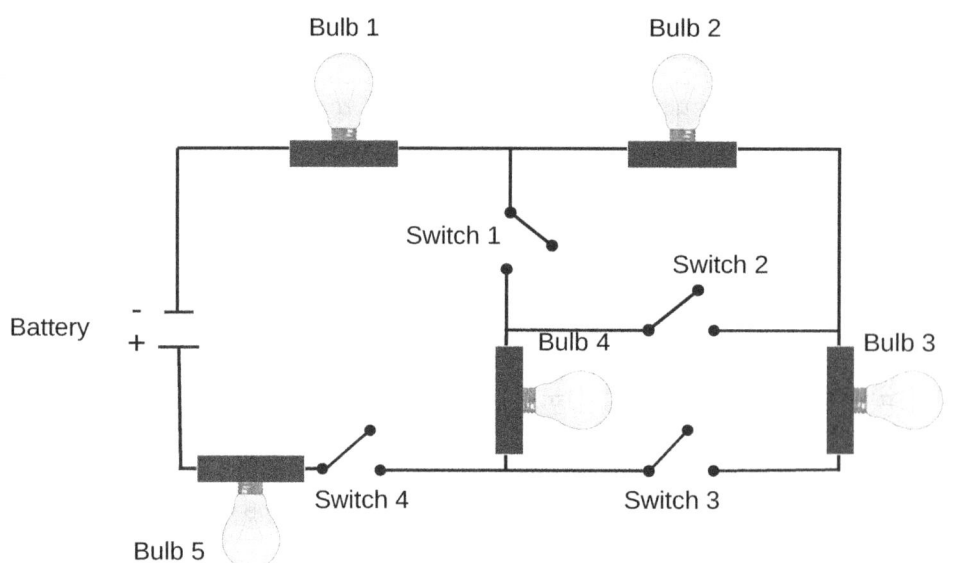

Answers Test Practice 2

1. A. 24 hours
2. D. Four
3. C. Evaporation, condensation, and precipitation.
4. A. Algae → insects → fish → turtles
5. B. Dolphin
6. B. The sunny window has warmer temperatures, which help the seed grow.
   A. Seeds need sunlight to make their food through photosynthesis.
7. B. Photosynthesis
8. A. Silk threads
9. C. Thermal energy from the sun.
10. D. Thermal energy from the hot soup.
11. C. Lightning generates sound waves.
12. C. A moving car
13. B. Liquid 2 has a lower density than liquid 1.
14. B. Gravity pulling the balloon downward.
15. B. They repel each other.
16. D. Allow the water to evaporate, leaving behind the sugar.
17. D. Allow the water to evaporate, leaving behind the ink.
18. B. Sample 2 is iron.
19. C. By revealing what kinds of plants and animals lived in an area.
20. C. Both are carved out by chemical weathering.
21. B. Mercury is the first planet, and Venus is the second.
22. B. The ink dissolved in the water.
23. B. Arctic Tundra
24. B. The Earth tilts on its axis, causing more direct sunlight in one hemisphere.
25. C. Tropical rainforests with high humidity and abundant vegetation.
26. A. Clouds
27. D. One of the blocks is less dense than the other three.
28. C. Disruption of local wildlife habitats.
29. B. Leaf shape
    D. Root color
30. B. Light passes through a magnifying glass.
31. A. Earth revolves around the sun.
32. A. Red giants are larger than white dwarfs.
    B. White dwarfs are hotter than red giants.
33. B. Earth's atmosphere distorts the light from stars.
34. A. A galaxy that includes our solar system.
35. B. Earth has a thick atmosphere with oxygen.
36. A. Mice live in a wider range of habitats, including forests, grasslands, agricultural areas, and urban settings, while squirrels are primarily found in areas with trees.
    C. Mice have a more diverse diet that includes seeds, grains, fruits, and insects, while squirrels primarily eat nuts, seeds, and fruits.
37. C. To capture sunlight for photosynthesis.
38. B. A fast-flowing river with rocky rapids and waterfalls.
39. B. Decrease the steepness of the hill.
40. C. Electrical energy
41. A. Kinetic energy
42. C. Mechanical energy
43. A. Measure the speed of descent for parachutes of different sizes. Conduct three trials for each parachute.
44. NONE

PRACTICE TEST 3

GET STARTED →

1. The Earth revolves around the Sun. What shape is the Earth's orbit around the Sun?

(A) Circular

(B) Elliptical

(C) Rectangular

(D) Triangular

2. What is the largest planet in our solar system by diameter?

(A) Jupiter

(B) Saturn

(C) Uranus

(D) Neptune

3. What is the most abundant gas in the Earth's atmosphere?

(A) Oxygen

(B) Carbon Dioxide

(C) Nitrogen

(D) Argon

4. Which of the following food chains correctly shows the flow of energy in a grassland ecosystem?

- A Grass → rabbits → foxes → eagles
- B Eagles → foxes → rabbits → grass
- C Rabbits → eagles → foxes → grass
- D Grass → foxes → eagles → rabbits

5. What is the main cause of global warming?

- A Volcanic eruptions and other natural phenomena.
- B Natural climate cycles that warm and cool the Earth.
- C Increased levels of greenhouse gases from human activities.
- D Solar flares, electromagnetic radiation, and similar energies.

6. In a desert ecosystem, what is the primary source of energy?

- A Cacti
- B Insects
- C Birds
- D Sunlight

7. How do plants primarily obtain carbon dioxide for photosynthesis?

(A) Through their roots.

(B) Through their leaves.

(C) Through their stems.

(D) Through their flowers.

8. Students observe a chicken life cycle diagram. What is the first stage in the life cycle of a chicken?

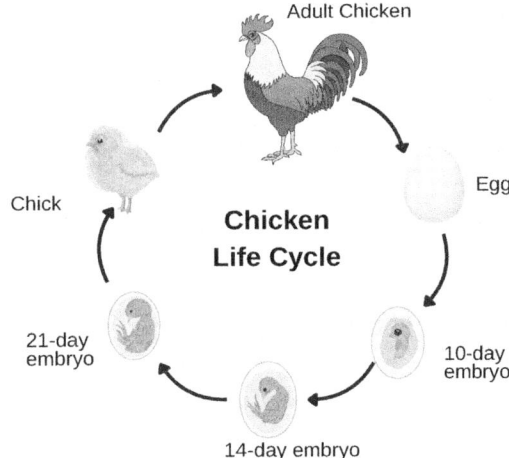

(A) Chick

(B) Adult

(C) Egg

(D) Embryo

9. During a thunderstorm, a student sees a flash of lightning. Which form of energy causes the lightning to occur?

(A) Mechanical energy from wind.

(B) Electrical energy from clouds.

(C) Chemical energy from rainwater.

(D) Thermal energy from the Sun.

10. During a foggy night walk, a student noticed the reflection of the street lights on the fog. What is the reason the light from the lamp becomes more visible in the fog?

(A) The fog particles reflect the light.

(B) The light is absorbed by the fog particles.

(C) The light passes through fog without any interaction.

(D) The light from the lamp changes color in the fog.

11. Which of the following objects would have the most kinetic energy?

(A) A car parked in a garage.

(B) A bicycle leaning against a wall.

(C) A rolling soccer ball.

(D) A rock resting on the ground.

12. Which type of energy is produced by vibrating objects?

(A) Electrical energy

(B) Chemical energy

(C) Sound energy

(D) Nuclear energy

13. Students observe the picture below where particles of an unknown material are added to pure water. After mixing, the particles float to the top of the container.

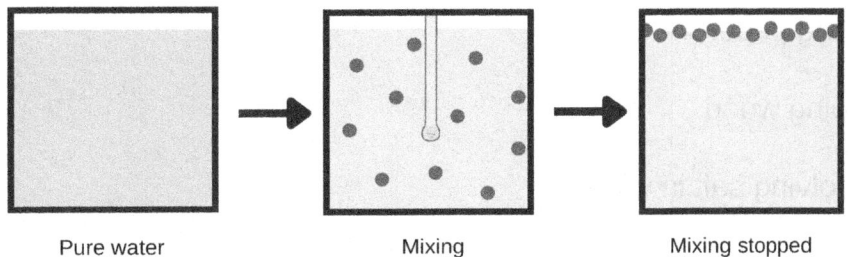

Pure water   Mixing   Mixing stopped

Which conclusion can be made from image?

(A) The particles have a higher density than water.

(B) The particles have a lower density than water.

(C) The particles have the same density as water.

(D) The particles are soluble in water.

14. Which of these materials would be the best conductor of electricity?

(A) Rubber

(B) Plastic

(C) Copper

(D) Wood

15. What is the purpose of a switch in an electrical circuit?

(A) To store electricity.

(B) To control the flow of electricity.

(C) To measure electricity.

(D) To generate electricity.

47

16. Which of the following is an example of a chemical change?

(A) Melting ice

(B) Cutting paper

(C) Burning wood

(D) Dissolving salt in water

17. A student prepares a mixture of tea leaves and water. What is the fastest way for the student to separate the tea leaves from the water?

(A) Use a magnet to attract the tea leaves.

(B) Heat the mixture until the tea leaves settle at the bottom.

(C) Pour the mixture through filter paper.

(D) Allow the water to evaporate, leaving behind the tea leaves.

18. A table of the properties of four different samples of matter is shown.

Sample	Conducts Electricity	Conducts Heat	Soluble in Water	Physical State at Room Temperature
1	No	No	No	Solid
2	Yes	Yes	No	Solid
3	No	Yes	Yes	Liquid
4	Yes	Yes	No	Liquid

Which answer is correct for sample 3?

(A) Sample 3 is plastic.

(B) Sample 3 is iron.

(C) Sample 3 is alcohol.

(D) Sample 3 is oxygen.

19. How are fossils typically formed?

(A) When plants or animals are buried quickly by sediment.

(B) When plants or animals dry out in the sun.

(C) When organisms are frozen in ice.

(D) When organisms decompose completely.

20. Deltas and estuaries are coastal landforms shaped by water. Which statement best describes how deltas and estuaries are similar?

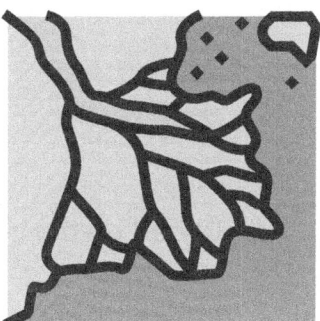

(A) Both are formed by glacial erosion.

(B) Both are influenced by tidal currents.

(C) Both are results of volcanic eruptions.

(D) Both are affected by seismic activity.

21. What is the Sun mainly made of?

(A) Rock

(B) Ice

(C) Gas

(D) Metal

22. A student compares the flow of water through four different types of sand. The setup and results of the investigation are shown in the table.

The student used this procedure to perform the investigation:

1. Place 100 grams of each type of sand into one of the funnels with a coffee filter.
2. Slowly pour 100 milliliters of water onto the sand in each funnel.
3. Allow the water in each funnel to drain for 30 minutes.
4. Record the amount of water in each beaker.
5. Subtract the amount of water in each beaker from 100 mL and record this number as the amount remaining in the funnel.

Sand Investigation Results

Type of Sand	Volume of Water Added (mL)	Water Collected in Beaker	Water Remaining in Funnel
Beach Sand	100	20	80
Desert Sand	100	49	51
River Sand	100	76	24
Volcanic Sand	100	19	81

Based on the investigation's results, answer the questions below.

Which type of sand retained the most water after 30 minutes?

A Beach Sand

B Desert Sand

C River Sand

D Volcanic Sand

23. Please refer to the previous question. Which type of sand allowed the most water to pass through into the beaker?

(A) Beach Sand

(B) Desert Sand

(C) River Sand

(D) Volcanic Sand

24. A student drew the following pictures to show the day-night cycle of Earth.

Sunrise: 6:15 AM
Sunset: 7:15 PM

Based on the pictures, how many hours of the daytime is in a day-night cycle?

(A) 12 hours

(B) 13 hours

(C) 14 hours

(D) 24 hours

25. Bengal tigers are large carnivorous cats known for their distinctive orange coat with black stripes. They primarily inhabit dense forests and grasslands, hunting large prey such as deer and wild boar.

Characteristics of Four Habitats

Habitat	Temperature	Yearly Precipitation	Soil
1	Hot and humid year-round	Heavy rainfall	Nutrient-rich soil
2	Moderate with distinct seasons	Evenly distributed rainfall	Loamy, fertile soil
3	Cold winters and mild summers	Low precipitation	Rocky, well-drained soil
4	Dry and arid year-round	Very low precipitation	Sandy, nutrient-poor soil

In which habitat would Bengal tigers be most likely to thrive?

A) Habitat 1

B) Habitat 2

C) Habitat 3

D) Habitat 4

26. A three-step process is shown:

Weathering → Erosion → Deposition

Which of these are most likely formed by the process shown?

A) Volcanic islands

B) River deltas

C) Craters

D) Metamorphic rocks

27. Which of the following materials is known for its hardness and is often used in cutting tools?

- (A) Wood
- (B) Diamond
- (C) Plastic
- (D) Clay

28. Which effect would most likely occur if a large shopping mall were built in an ecosystem?

- (A) Competition for food among animals would decrease.
- (B) Natural habitats for wildlife would be destroyed.
- (C) Noise pollution would decrease.
- (D) Water quality in nearby streams would improve.

29. Which of the following is a non-renewable resource?

- (A) Solar energy
- (B) Wind energy
- (C) Coal
- (D) Water

30. Which situations involve light being refracted? Select TWO correct answers.

(A) A student views a fish in an aquarium.

(B) Light passes through a prism, creating a spectrum.

(C) A student observes their reflection in a spoon.

(D) Sunlight passes through a window into a dark room.

(E) Light travels through a magnifying glass to ignite paper.

31. What is the primary reason why the moon appears to change shape throughout the month?

(A) The moon revolves around Earth.

(B) The moon rotates on its axis.

(C) Earth rotates on its axis.

(D) The Sun revolves around Earth.

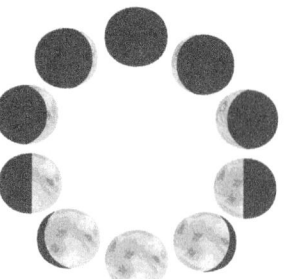

32. A student is studying the characteristics of planets and stars. Which statements about planets and stars are correct? Select TWO correct answers.

(A) Planets orbit stars.

(B) Stars are typically smaller than planets.

(C) Stars produce light, while planets reflect light.

(D) Planets are made entirely of gases.

(E) Both planets and stars have the same temperature.

54

33. A student is learning about the phases of the moon. Which of the following shows the correct sequence of the moon's phases?

- (A) New moon, waxing crescent, first quarter, full moon
- (B) Full moon, third quarter, waning crescent, new moon
- (C) First quarter, waxing crescent, full moon, new moon
- (D) Full moon, waxing crescent, first quarter, new moon

34. A student observes a solar eclipse. What is happening during a solar eclipse?

- (A) The Earth is between the Sun and the moon.
- (B) The moon is between the Sun and the Earth.
- (C) The Sun is between the Earth and the moon.
- (D) The moon and the Sun are on opposite sides of Earth.

35. What is the smallest unit of an element that still has the properties of that element?

- (A) Atom
- (B) Molecule
- (C) Compound
- (D) Cell

36. This question has two parts. First, answer Part A. Then, answer Part B.

Part A

A student observes two animals: a lion and a cheetah. Which statement BEST describes a key difference between lions and cheetahs?

(A) Cheetahs are social animals that live in prides and hunt cooperatively, while lions are solitary hunters.

(B) Lions have spots on their fur for camouflage in grasslands, while cheetahs have a distinct coat pattern for identification.

(C) Lions hunt by stalking their prey and ambushing it in groups, while cheetahs rely on their speed for chasing and catching prey.

(D) Lions have retractable claws for climbing trees, while cheetahs have non-retractable claws for gripping the ground.

Part B

Based on your answer to Part A, which statement BEST explains a potential disadvantage of the behavior or adaptation described?

(A) Lions' ability to camouflage helps them blend into their surroundings to surprise prey.

(B) Cheetahs' reliance on speed makes them vulnerable to injuries during high-speed pursuits.

(C) Lions' stalking behavior requires them to expend more energy compared to cheetahs' quick bursts of speed.

(D) Cheetahs' solitary hunting makes them less efficient in taking down larger prey compared to the lions' cooperative efforts.

37. What do we call a community of living organisms and their physical environment?

(A) Environment

(B) Habitat

(C) Ecosystem

(D) Biome

56

38. A group of animals is shown.

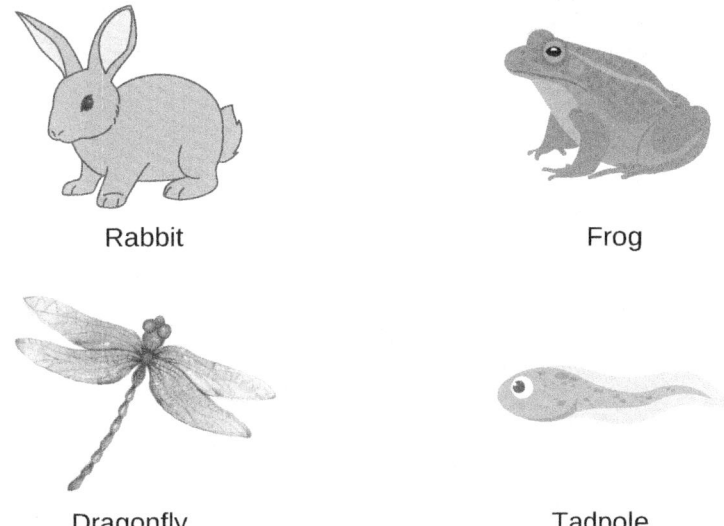

Rabbit

Frog

Dragonfly

Tadpole

Which habitat are these animals BEST suited for?

(A) A dense rainforest with tall trees and thick underbrush.

(B) A sandy desert with extreme temperature variations.

(C) A freshwater pond with aquatic plants and insects.

(D) A cold mountain stream with rocky banks.

39. Students are experimenting with different slopes for their toy cars. The cars start from rest at the top of the ramp. What change to the ramp slope will reduce the force required to move the cars?

(A) Decrease the steepness of the ramp.

(B) Increase the steepness of the ramp.

(C) Add weight to the toy cars.

(D) Use a longer ramp.

40. When you throw a ball into the air, what force brings it back down to the ground?

- A Air resistance
- B Magnetism
- C Gravity
- D Friction

41. When you push a swing, what force brings it back towards you after it swings away?

- A Magnetism
- B Gravity
- C Air resistance
- D Tension

42. Students want to investigate how the height of a ramp affects the distance a toy car travels. Which procedure should they follow for their experiment?

- A Measure the distance traveled by the toy car using ramps of different heights. Conduct three trials for each height.
- B Measure the distance traveled by three different toy cars using the same ramp height. Conduct trials for each car.
- C Measure the distance traveled by the toy car on different surfaces using the same ramp height. Conduct three trials for each surface.
- D Measure the distance traveled by the toy car on the same ramp height by different students. Conduct three trials for each student.

43. The circuit has five lightbulbs and four switches. If Switch 1 and 4 are closed, which lightbulbs will glow? Write the answer on the line provided. If none of the lightbulbs will glow, write NONE on the line: _____

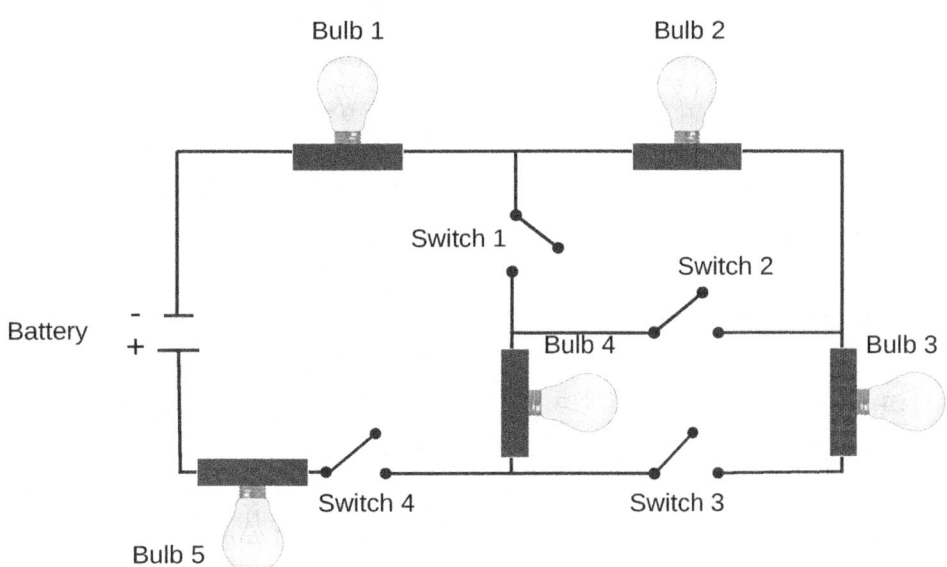

44. What happens when a ball is dropped on a hard surface?

(A) It stops immediately.

(B) It continues to bounce indefinitely.

(C) It bounces back due to elastic force.

(D) It rolls away.

Answers Practice Test 3

1. B. Elliptical
2. A. Jupiter
3. C. Nitrogen
4. A. Grass → rabbits → foxes → eagles
5. C. Increased levels of greenhouse gases from human activities.
6. D. Sunlight
7. B. Through their leaves.
8. C. Egg
9. B. Electrical energy from clouds.
10. A. The fog particles reflect the light.
11. C. A rolling soccer ball.
12. C. Sound energy
13. B. The particles have a lower density than water.
14. C. Copper
15. B. To control the flow of electricity.
16. C. Burning wood
17. C. Pour the mixture through filter paper.
18. C. Sample 3 is alcohol.
19. A. When plants or animals are buried quickly by sediment.
20. B. Both are influenced by tidal currents.
21. C. Gas
22. Question 1: D. Volcanic Sand
23. C. River sand
24. B. 13 hours
25. A. Habitat 1
26. C. River deltas
27. B. Diamond

28. B. Natural habitats for wildlife would be destroyed.
29. C. Coal
30. B. Light passes through a prism, creating a spectrum.
    C. A student observes their reflection in a spoon.
31. A. The moon revolves around Earth.
32. A. Planets orbit stars.
    C. Stars produce light, while planets reflect light.
33. A. New moon, waxing crescent, first quarter, full moon
34. B. The moon is between the sun and the Earth.
35. A. Atom
36. C. Lions hunt by stalking their prey and ambushing it in groups, while cheetahs rely on their speed for chasing and catching prey.
    D. Cheetahs' solitary hunting makes them less efficient in taking down larger prey compared to the lions' cooperative efforts.
37. C. Ecosystem
38. A. A dense rainforest with tall trees and thick underbrush.
39. C. Add weight to the toy cars
40. C. Gravity
41. B. Gravity
42. A. Measure the distance traveled by the toy car using ramps of different heights. Conduct three trials for each height.
43. Bulbs 1 and 5.
44. C. It bounces back due to elastic force.

60

PRACTICE TEST 4

GET STARTED →

1. What is the smallest planet in our solar system by diameter?

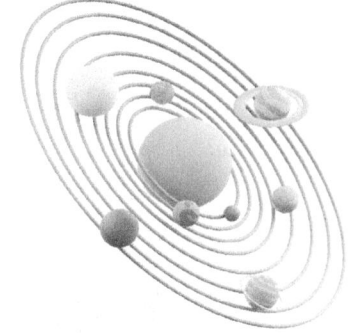

(A) Mercury

(B) Venus

(C) Mars

(D) Pluto

2. The Earth has a natural satellite. What is it called?

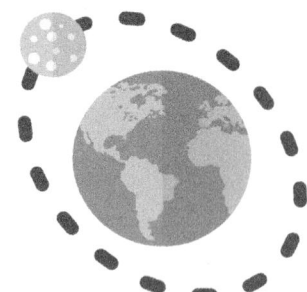

(A) Sun

(B) Mars

(C) Moon

(D) Venus

3. Which force keeps the Earth in orbit around the Sun?

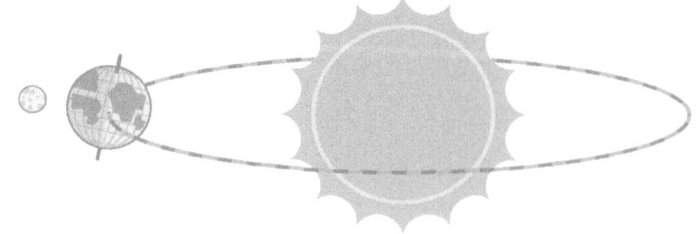

(A) Electromagnetic force

(B) Gravitational force

(C) Nuclear force

(D) Frictional force

4. Why do you think some animals have bright colors?

- (A) To hide from predators.
- (B) To attract mates.
- (C) To scare away prey.
- (D) To camouflage.

5. Why do you think plants have different types of leaves (e.g., broad, needle-like, spiky)?

- (A) To make them look interesting.
- (B) To help them catch insects.
- (C) To adapt to different environments.
- (D) To scare away animals.

6. In a grassland ecosystem, what is the primary source of energy?

- (A) Bison
- (B) Grass
- (C) Birds
- (D) Wind

7. Answer the question with the help of the following image. What gas is released into the atmosphere as a byproduct of photosynthesis?

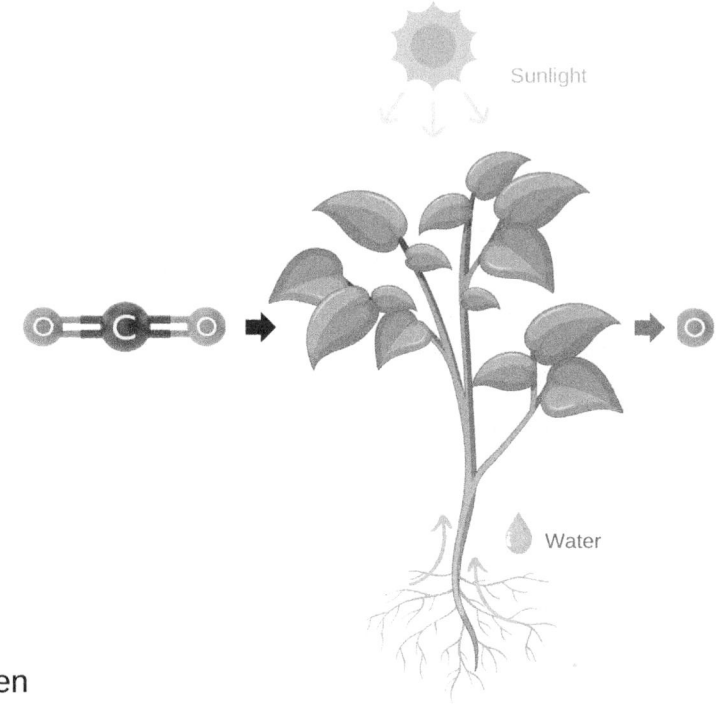

- (A) Oxygen
- (B) Nitrogen
- (C) Carbon dioxide
- (D) Methane

8. Students observe a diagram showing the life cycle of ferns. Where do ferns produce their spores?

- (A) On the leaves.
- (B) In flowers.
- (C) In cones.
- (D) On the stems.

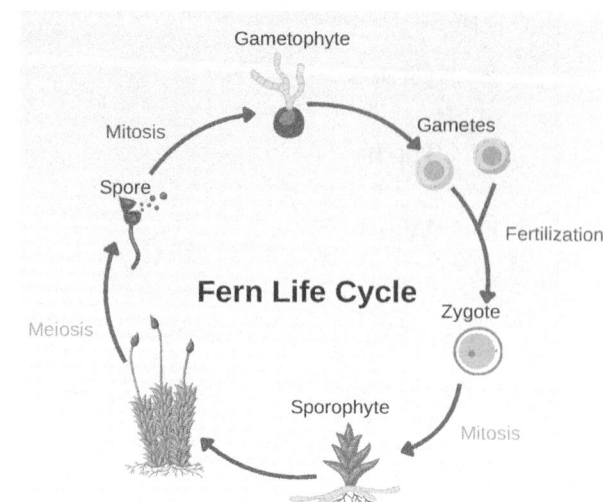

9. A student rubs two sticks together to start a fire while camping. Which type of energy is primarily responsible for igniting the sticks?

A Nuclear energy from the ground.

B Electrical energy from a nearby generator.

C Chemical energy from friction.

D Thermal energy from the air.

10. How does a trampoline demonstrate elastic force?

A By absorbing sound.

B By storing energy and bouncing back.

C By attracting objects.

D By conducting electricity.

11. Students observe the image below where two different liquids are poured into the same container. Which conclusion can be made from the image?

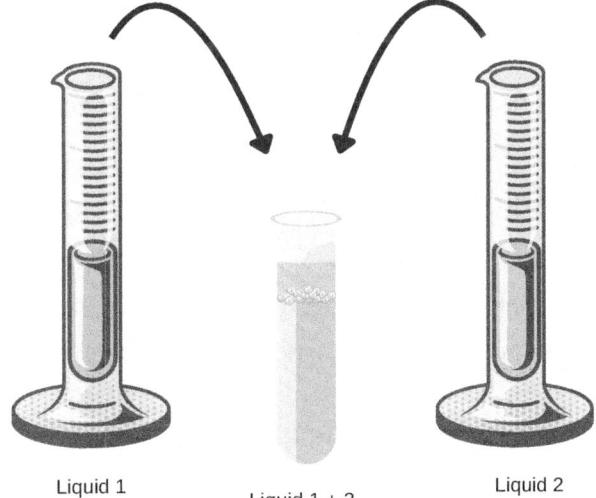

Liquid 1

Liquid 1 + 2

Liquid 2

A The different liquids could be water and oil.

B The different liquids could be water and alcohol.

C Liquid 1 is soluble in liquid 2.

D Two different liquids could be water and dishwashing soap.

65

12. This question has two parts. First, answer Part A. Then, based on your answer to Part A, answer Part B.

Part A

A student examines two plants: a dandelion and an oak tree. Which statement BEST describes a key difference between dandelions and oak trees in their reproduction?

- (A) Dandelions reproduce through seeds that disperse in the wind, while oak trees reproduce through acorns that fall to the ground.
- (B) Dandelions reproduce through acorns that fall to the ground, while oak trees reproduce through seeds that disperse in the wind.
- (C) Dandelions and oak trees reproduce through spores released from their leaves, but dandelions grow faster in moist soil.
- (D) Dandelions and oak trees are similar in reproduction methods, but dandelions have broader leaves that capture more sunlight for photosynthesis.

Part B

Based on your answer to Part A, which statement BEST explains how this difference in reproduction helps each plant species survive?

- (A) Dandelions' ability to disperse seeds in the wind allows them to colonize new areas quickly and compete with other plants for resources.
- (B) Oak trees' production of acorns provides a food source for animals such as squirrels and deer, ensuring widespread seed dispersal.
- (C) Dandelions' slow growth does not allow them to spread seeds fast compared to oak trees.
- (D) Oak trees' needle-like leaves capture less sunlight, making them unable to grow taller and overshadow other plants in dense forest environments.

13. Which of the following is a characteristic of acids?

- (A) Sour taste.
- (B) Bitter taste.
- (C) Slippery feel.
- (D) Red litmus paper turns blue.

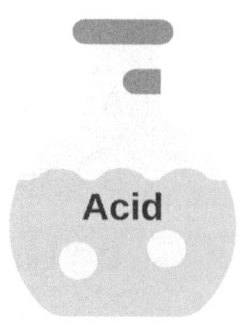

Acid

14. If you place a cold spoon in a hot cup of soup, what will happen to the temperature of the spoon and the soup?

A The spoon will get colder, and the soup will stay the same.

B The spoon will get warmer, and the soup will get cooler.

C The spoon and soup will both get warmer.

D The spoon and soup will both get cooler.

15. In a recycling project, a student mixes plastic beads and metal screws. How can the student separate the plastic beads from the metal screws?

A Dissolve the mixture in water and then filter it.

B Use a magnet to attract the metal screws.

C Heat the mixture until the plastic beads melt.

D Pour the mixture through filter paper to separate.

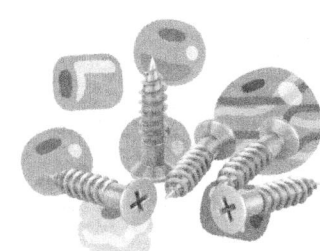

16. A table of the properties of four different samples of matter is shown.

Sample	Conducts Electricity	Conducts Heat	Soluble in Water	Physical State at Room Temperature
1	No	No	No	Solid
2	Yes	Yes	No	Solid
3	No	Yes	Yes	Liquid
4	Yes	Yes	No	Liquid

Which answer is correct for sample 4?

A Sample 4 is plastic.

B Sample 4 is iron.

C Sample 4 is alcohol.

D Sample 4 is mercury.

17. What is the main characteristic of mammals?

(A) They lay eggs.

(B) They have hair or fur and produce milk for their young.

(C) They have scales.

(D) They can fly.

18. Plateaus and buttes are elevated landforms found in various regions. Which statement best describes how plateaus and buttes are similar?

(A) Both are formed by volcanic ash deposits.

(B) Both are shaped by uplift and erosion.

(C) Both are remnants of ancient sea beds.

(D) Both are results of underground lava flows.

19. In modern astronomy, scientists study Earth and Mars using advanced telescopes. What are the positions of these planets in relation to the Sun?

(A) Earth is the planet closest to the Sun, and Mars is the second planet from the Sun.

(B) Earth is the second planet from the Sun, and Mars is the third planet from the Sun.

(C) Mars is the planet closest to the Sun, and Earth is the second planet from the Sun.

(D) Earth is the third planet from the Sun, and Mars is the fourth planet from the Sun.

20. A student stirred a sugar cube into a cup of hot coffee. After stirring, the student noticed that the coffee tasted sweeter. What most likely happened to the sugar cube?

A The sugar cube turned into steam and disappeared.

B The sugar cube broke into smaller pieces.

C The sugar cube dissolved in the coffee.

D The sugar cube sank to the bottom of the cup.

21. Imagine you are studying a plant species found in wetlands. You observe the following characteristics:

- Broad, flat leaves
- Extensive root system
- Ability to float on water
- White flowers that bloom at night
- Seeds dispersed by water currents

Based on these characteristics, which habitat do you think this plant is most likely adapted to live in?

A Desert

B Rainforest

C Wetlands

D Grassland

22. Why do days and nights have almost equal length during the equinoxes?

A The Earth's axis is perpendicular to its orbit around the Sun.

B The Earth is closest to the Sun during the equinoxes.

C The Moon is in a specific position that balances day and night.

D The Sun's energy is equally distributed around the Earth during the equinoxes.

23. Polar bears are large carnivorous mammals known for their thick fur and ability to survive in harsh cold climates. In which habitat are polar bears most likely to be found?

(A) Tropical rainforests with dense vegetation.

(B) Arctic regions with sea ice and tundra.

(C) Deserts with extreme temperatures and sparse vegetation.

(D) Grasslands with moderate temperatures and open plains.

24. A three-step process is shown:

Uplift → Weathering → Erosion

Which of these are most likely formed by the process shown?

(A) Fossils

(B) Mountains

(C) Valleys

(D) Lava flows

25. Why do you think some substances dissolve in water while others do not?

(A) Because they like to stay dry.

(B) Because they are afraid of water.

(C) Because they are made of different molecules.

(D) Because they want to hide.

26. What would most likely happen if a forest area was cleared to build residential housing?

- (A) Biodiversity in the area would increase.
- (B) Soil erosion would decrease.
- (C) Animal migration routes would be disrupted.
- (D) Water levels in local rivers would rise.

27. Students observe different types of birds in a wetland. They focus on ducks and record their characteristics:

Duck Characteristics:
- Webbed feet for swimming
- Waterproof feathers for floating
- Omnivorous diet of aquatic plants, insects, and small fish
- Nests near water in reeds or grasses
- Migration to warmer areas in winter

Why do ducks have webbed feet?

- (A) To climb trees.
- (B) To attract mates.
- (C) To swim and dive for food.
- (D) To dig burrows.

28. What do you think happens when you mix vinegar (acetic acid) and baking soda (sodium bicarbonate)?

- (A) They explode.
- (B) They turn into a solid.
- (C) They create bubbles and fizz.
- (D) They turn into water.

29. What causes the apparent movement of stars across the night sky?

- (A) Earth revolves around the Sun.
- (B) Earth rotates on its axis.
- (C) The Sun revolves around Earth.
- (D) Stars rotate on their axes.

30. A student is observing the characteristics of comets and asteroids. Which statements about comets and asteroids are correct? Select TWO correct answers.

- (A) Comets are primarily made of ice and dust.
- (B) Asteroids produce light like stars.
- (C) Both comets and asteroids orbit the Sun.
- (D) Comets are only found in the asteroid belt.
- (E) Asteroids have tails that grow when they approach the Sun.

31. A student is studying the planets in our solar system. Which statements about the planets are correct? Select TWO correct answers.

- (A) Mars is known as the Red Planet.
- (B) Jupiter is the smallest planet.
- (C) Venus has a surface covered with water.
- (D) Saturn is famous for its rings.
- (E) Mercury is the furthest planet from the Sun.

32. What causes day and night on Earth?

- (A) The Earth's rotation on its axis.
- (B) The Earth's orbit around the Sun.
- (C) The tilt of the Earth's axis.
- (D) The movement of the moon around Earth.

33. What is the primary reason we experience high and low tides on Earth?

- (A) The rotation of the Earth on its axis.
- (B) The gravitational pull of the Moon and the Sun on Earth's oceans.
- (C) The Earth's revolution around the Sun.
- (D) The wind patterns over the oceans.

34. What is the main difference between amphibians and reptiles?

- (A) Amphibians have feathers that are lost when they mature, and reptiles have scales all their lives.
- (B) Amphibians lay eggs only on dry land, and reptiles give birth to live young either in water or on land.
- (C) Amphibians have dry skin that does not require moisture, and reptiles have moist skin all of the time.
- (D) Amphibians usually have moist skin and live in water and on land, whereas reptiles have dry, scaly skin and live primarily on land.

35. How do you think plants and animals adapt to survive in different habitats?

    (A) By changing their colors.

    (B) By learning new skills.

    (C) By evolving physical traits.

    (D) By hiding from predators.

36. A group of animals is shown:

 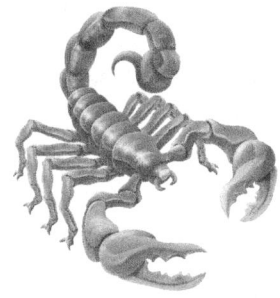 

Camel   Scorpion   Rattle Snake

Which habitat are these animals BEST suited for?

    (A) A temperate grassland with fertile soil and occasional trees.

    (B) A polar ice cap with frozen seas and little vegetation.

    (C) A hot desert with sandy soil and sparse vegetation.

    (D) A dense mangrove swamp with brackish water and tidal movements.

37. A group of students is testing how far they can throw different balls. What change will reduce the force needed to throw the balls the same distance?

    (A) Use a lighter ball.

    (B) Use a heavier ball.

    (C) Throw the ball at a higher angle.

    (D) Throw the ball at a lower angle.

74

38. When you ride a bike uphill, which force are you mostly working against?

- (A) Gravity
- (B) Air resistance
- (C) Magnetism
- (D) Friction

39. Which of these is an example of kinetic energy?

- (A) A battery-operated toy robot.
- (B) A ball thrown into the air.
- (C) A book sitting on a shelf.
- (D) A stretched rubber band.

40. The Falling Objects:

Emily and James are dropping objects from different heights to see how fast they fall.

Which object do you think will hit the ground first: a small ball or a big ball? Why?

- (A) The small ball, because it is lighter.
- (B) The big ball, because it is heavier.
- (C) Both balls will hit the ground at the same time.
- (D) It depends on how hard they are dropped.

_____

_____

_____

_____

_____

41. The circuit has five lightbulbs and four switches. If Switch 1, 2, and 4 are closed which lightbulbs will glow? Write the answer on the line provided. If none of the lightbulbs will glow, write NONE on the line: _____

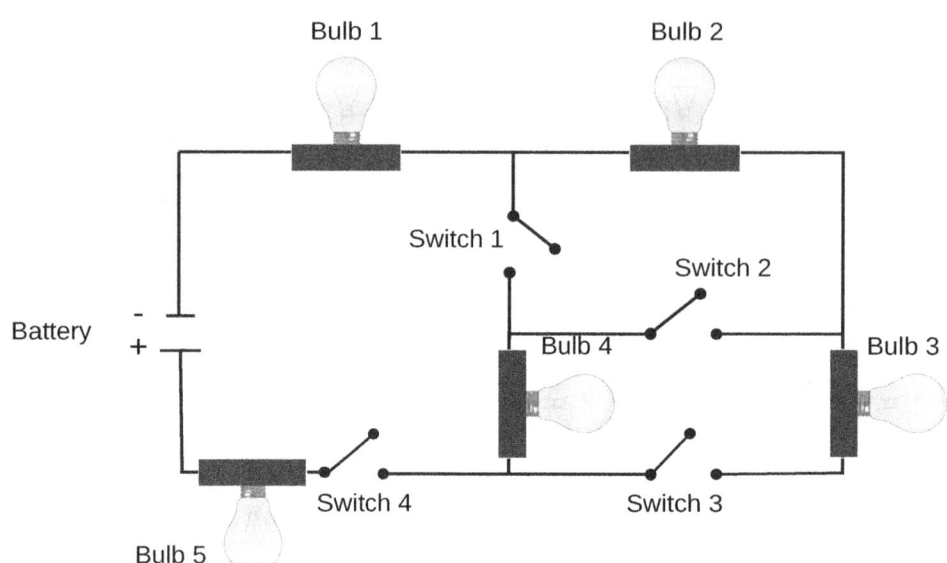

42. During a science experiment, students observe that a balloon rubbed against a wool sweater sticks to a wall. What is the most likely explanation for this phenomenon?

(A) The balloon becomes magnetic when rubbed against wool.

(B) The balloon gains a positive charge and is attracted to the negative charge on the wall.

(C) The balloon emits light that attracts it to the wall surface.

(D) The balloon absorbs moisture from the sweater, causing it to stick to the wall.

43. A student holds a flashlight in front of a mirror. What is the most likely explanation for why the student sees the light beam reflected off the mirror?

(A) The mirror absorbs the light beam.

(B) The mirror bends the light beam.

(C) The mirror transmits the light beam.

(D) The mirror reflects the light beam.

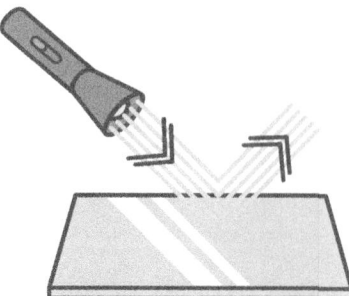

44. A student notices that the temperature decreases as they climb to the top of a mountain. What is the most likely reason for this temperature change?

A The mountain absorbs heat from the atmosphere.

B The mountain reflects heat from the Sun.

C The mountain refracts heat from the surroundings.

D The mountain experiences a decrease in air pressure, causing a decrease in temperature.

Answers Practice Test 4

1. A. Mercury
2. C. Moon
3. B. Gravitational force
4. B. To attract mates
5. C. To adapt to different environments.
6. B. Grass
7. A. Oxygen
8. A. On the leaves
9. D. Thermal energy from the air.
10. B. By storing energy and bouncing back.
11. A. Two different liquids could be water and oil.
12. A. Dandelions reproduce through seeds that disperse in the wind, while oak trees reproduce through acorns that fall to the ground.

   A. Dandelions' ability to disperse seeds in the wind allows them to colonize new areas quickly and compete with other plants for resources.
13. A. Sour taste
14. B. The spoon will get warmer, and the soup will get cooler.
15. B. Use a magnet to attract the metal screws.
16. D. Sample 4 is mercury.
17. B. They have hair or fur and produce milk for their young.
18. B. Both are shaped by uplift and erosion.
19. D. Earth is the third planet from the Sun, and Mars is the fourth planet from the Sun.
20. C. The sugar cube dissolved in the coffee.
21. C. Wetlands
22. A. The Earth's axis is perpendicular to its orbit around the Sun.
23. B. Arctic regions with sea ice and tundra.
24. C. Valleys
25. C. Because they are made of different molecules.
26. C. Animal migration routes would be disrupted.
27. C. To swim and dive for food.
28. C. They create bubbles and fizz.

29. B. Earth rotates on its axis.
30. A. Comets are primarily made of ice and dust.
    C. Both comets and asteroids orbit the sun.
31. A. Mars is known as the Red Planet.
    D. Saturn is famous for its rings.
32. A. The Earth's rotation on its axis.
33. B. The gravitational pull of the Moon and the Sun on Earth's oceans.
34. D. Amphibians usually have moist skin and live in water and on land, whereas reptiles have dry, scaly skin and live primarily on land.
35. C. By evolving physical traits.
36. C. A hot desert with sandy soil and sparse vegetation.
37. A. Use a lighter ball.
38. A. Gravity
39. B. A ball thrown into the air.
40. C. Both balls will hit the ground at the same time.
Explanation: In physics, all objects fall towards the Earth at the same rate of acceleration due to gravity (approximately 9.8 meters per second squared). Therefore, regardless of their size or weight (assuming air resistance is negligible), both the small ball and the big ball will hit the ground at the same time when dropped from the same height. This scenario introduces the concept of gravity and how it affects falling objects in a straightforward manner.
41. Bulbs 1, 2, and 5.
42. B. The balloon gains a positive charge and is attracted to the negative charge on the wall.
43. D. The mirror reflects the light beam.
44. D. The mountain experiences a decrease in air pressure, causing a decrease in temperature.

PRACTICE TEST 5

GET STARTED →

1. Which planet in our solar system is known for having the most extensive and complex system of rings?

    (A) Saturn

    (B) Jupiter

    (C) Uranus

    (D) Neptune

2. What is the primary energy source for the Earth's climate and weather systems?

    (A) The Moon

    (B) The Sun

    (C) The Earth's core

    (D) The Earth's magnetic field

3. Which ocean is the largest by surface area?

    (A) Atlantic Ocean

    (B) Indian Ocean

    (C) Arctic Ocean

    (D) Pacific Ocean

4. Which of the following food chains correctly shows the flow of energy in a tundra ecosystem?

(A) Lichens → caribou → wolves → polar bears

(B) Polar bears → wolves → caribou → lichens

(C) Caribou → polar bears → wolves → lichens

(D) Lichens → wolves → polar bears → caribou

5. How does deforestation affect the environment?

(A) Increases biodiversity.

(B) Reduces carbon dioxide in the atmosphere.

(C) Leads to loss of habitat, reduces biodiversity, and contributes to climate change.

(D) Improves soil quality.

6. In a deep-sea hydrothermal vent ecosystem, what is the primary source of energy?

(A) Crabs

(B) Bacteria

(C) Fish

(D) Waves

7. Answer the question with the help of the following image. During photosynthesis, which gas is typically consumed and converted, leading to its release as a byproduct into the atmosphere?

A) Oxygen

B) Nitrogen

C) Carbon dioxide

D) Methane

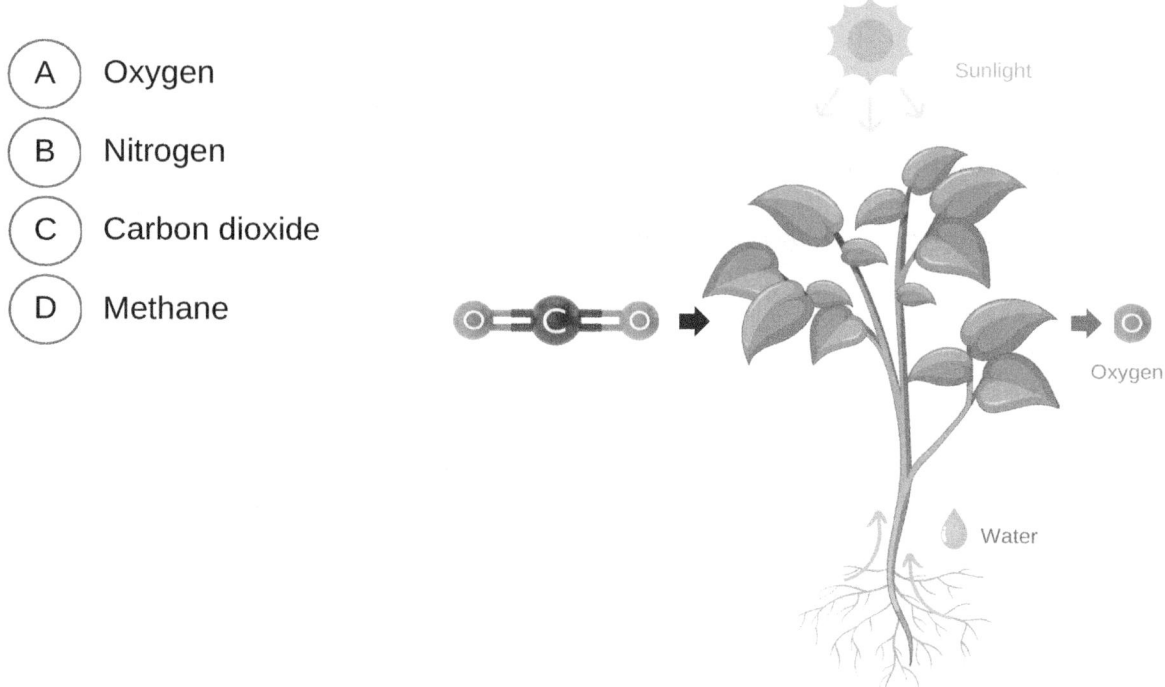

8. With the help of the image answer the question. What is the process called when tadpoles transform into adult frogs?

A) Metamorphosis

B) Evolution

C) Adaptation

D) Molt

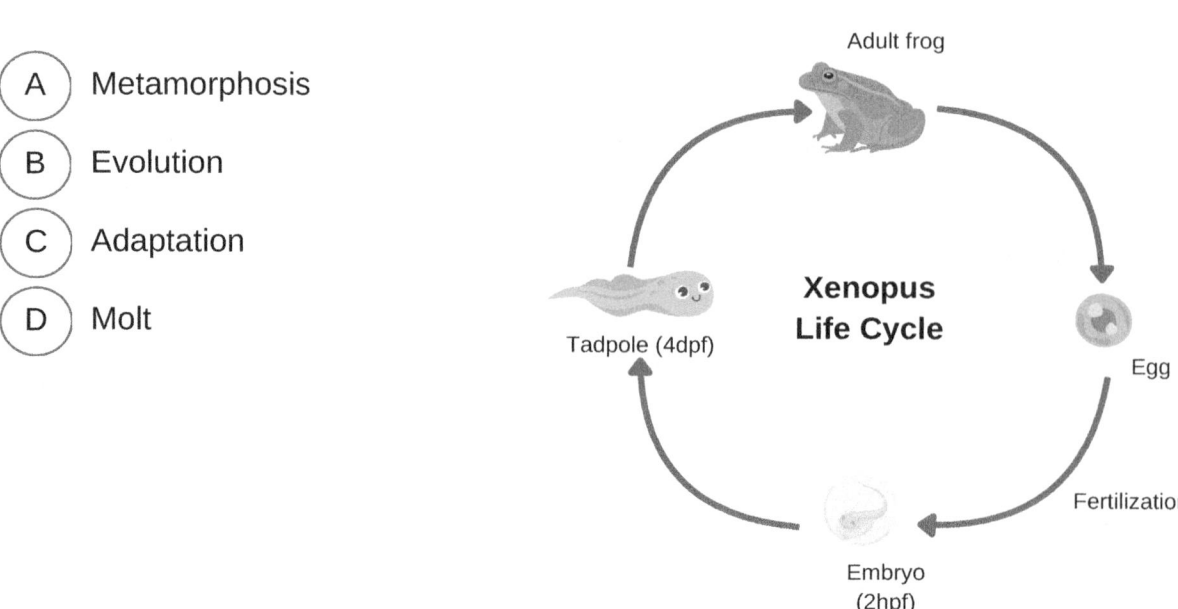

9. In a science experiment, a student observes water boiling in a kettle on a stove. Which form of energy is directly heating the water?

- (A) Mechanical energy from the stove burner.
- (B) Electrical energy from the power outlet.
- (C) Chemical energy from the water molecules.
- (D) Thermal energy from the stove burner.

10. During a demonstration, a teacher shined a laser beam through a smoke-filled room. What is the reason the laser beam becomes visible in the smoke?

- (A) The smoke particles reflect the laser light.
- (B) The laser light is absorbed by the smoke.
- (C) The laser light passes through without any interaction.
- (D) Smoke makes laser beams change color.

11. A book falls off a table and lands on the floor. What force causes the book to come to rest?

- (A) Air resistance pushing against the book.
- (B) Gravity pulling the book downward.
- (C) Friction between the book and the floor.
- (D) Elastic force from the impact of hitting the floor.

12. Students observe the picture below where particles of an unknown material are added to pure water. After mixing, the particles float in the container.

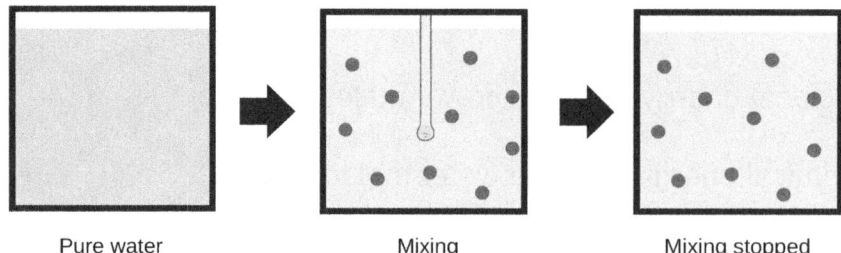

Pure water   Mixing   Mixing stopped

Which conclusion can be made from the image?

(A)   Water has a higher density than the particles'.

(B)   Water has a lower density than the particles'.

(C)   Water has a similar density to the particles'.

(D)   The particles are partially soluble in water.

13. The Balloon Race:

Sarah and Tom are blowing up balloons and racing them across the room.

Balloon A: This balloon is blown up with a small amount of air.
Balloon B: This balloon is blown up with a large amount of air.

Which balloon do you think will move faster across the room: Balloon A or Balloon B? Why?

(A)   Balloon A, because it has less air.

(B)   Balloon B, because it has more air.

(C)   Both balloons will move at the same speed.

(D)   It depends on how Sarah and Tom blow up the balloons.

_____

_____

_____

_____

14. How do you think soap helps clean dirty dishes?

    (A) By making them smell nice.

    (B) By breaking up dirt and grease into smaller pieces.

    (C) By coloring them.

    (D) By making them float.

15. A student combines a mixture of sand and salt. How can the student separate the sand and salt?

    (A) Dissolve the mixture in water and then filter it.

    (B) Use a magnet to attract the sand particles.

    (C) Heat the mixture until the sand burns away.

    (D) Pour the mixture through filter paper to separate.

16. The Melting Race:

Sarah and Tom are conducting an experiment to see which substance melts faster.

Substance A: A small piece of butter.
Substance B: A small piece of chocolate.

Which substance do you think will melt faster: Substance A (butter) or Substance B (chocolate)? Why?

    (A) Substance A, because it is softer.

    (B) Substance B, because it is sweeter.

    (C) Both substances will melt at the same rate.

    (D) It depends on the temperature of the room.

_____

_____

_____

_____

17. A table of the properties of four different samples of matter is shown.

Sample	Conducts Electricity	Conducts Heat	Soluble in Water	Physical State at Room Temperature
1	No	No	Yes	Solid
2	Yes	Yes	No	Solid
3	No	Yes	Yes	Liquid
4	No	Yes	Yes	Gas

Which answer is correct for sample 4?

- (A) Sample 4 is plastic.
- (B) Sample 4 is iron.
- (C) Sample 4 is alcohol.
- (D) Sample 4 is oxygen.

18. Which of the following animals is cold-blooded?

Lizard   Dog   Bird   Dolphin

- (A) Lizard
- (B) Dog
- (C) Bird
- (D) Dolphin

19. Fjord and Inlet:

Fjords and inlets are water features along coastal regions. Which statement best describes how fjords and inlets are similar?

(A) Both are formed by sedimentary rock deposits.

(B) Both are created by glacial erosion.

(C) Both are results of tectonic plate movements.

(D) Both are influenced by river deltas.

20. Which of the following correctly describes the position of Jupiter and Saturn in the solar system?

(A) Jupiter is closer to the Sun than Saturn.

(B) Saturn is closer to the Sun than Jupiter.

(C) Jupiter and Saturn are the closest planets to the Sun.

(D) Saturn is the closest planet to the Sun.

21. A student spilled colored dye onto a white fabric and then rinsed it under cold water. After rinsing, the fabric was no longer white but had taken on the color of the dye. What most likely happened to the dye?

(A) The dye evaporated from the fabric.

(B) The dye dissolved in the water.

(C) The dye solidified on the fabric.

(D) The dye was absorbed into the fabric's fibers.

22. Imagine you are studying a reptile species. You observe the following characteristics:

- Pale coloration to reflect sunlight
- Long, slender body with scales
- Efficient kidneys to conserve water
- Burrows underground during the day
- Diet primarily consists of insects and small rodents.

Based on these characteristics, which habitat do you think this reptile is most likely adapted to live in?

- (A) Rainforest
- (B) Desert
- (C) Arctic Tundra
- (D) Grassland

23. Why do we experience shorter days in the winter?

- (A) The Earth tilts away from the Sun, resulting in less direct sunlight.
- (B) The Earth moves further away from the Sun during winter.
- (C) The Moon blocks part of the sunlight during winter.
- (D) The Earth spins faster during winter.

24. Water lilies are aquatic plants known for their floating leaves and vibrant flowers. In which aquatic environment are water lilies most likely to thrive?

- (A) Fast-flowing rivers with rocky bottoms.
- (B) Shallow ponds with muddy bottoms.
- (C) Deep lakes with sandy bottoms.
- (D) Salty marshes with brackish water.

25. A three-step process is shown:

Heat → Pressure → Recrystallization

Which of these are most likely formed by the process shown?

A Clouds

B Metamorphic rocks

C Water

D Glaciers

26. What property makes metals like aluminum and copper useful for making cooking utensils?

A They are brittle.

B They are heavy.

C They conduct heat well.

D They are transparent.

27. What would most likely be the environmental impact of expanding agricultural fields into a wetland area?

A Improved water quality in the wetland.

B Reduced habitats for wetland species.

C Increased biodiversity in the area.

D Decreased need for irrigation.

28. Students are learning about the different animals in a zoo. They focus on giraffes and record their characteristics:

Giraffe Characteristics:
- Long neck and legs for reaching high leaves
- Coat with patches of brown spots for camouflage
- Herbivorous diet primarily of leaves and buds
- Large, heart-shaped tongue for grasping leaves
- Habitat in savannas with dry grasslands and scattered trees

What is the most likely reason giraffes have a long neck?

A) To run faster.

B) To hide from predators.

C) To reach high leaves.

D) To swim in rivers.

29. Which object will float in water?

A) Wooden block.

B) Metal coin.

C) Plastic toy.

D) Rock.

30. If you drop a feather and a hammer on the Moon, where there is no air resistance, what will happen?

A) The feather will fall slower than the hammer.

B) The hammer will fall slower than the feather.

C) Both will fall at the same rate.

D) The hammer will float while the feather falls.

31. A student is studying the properties of different celestial bodies. Which statements about celestial bodies are correct? Select TWO correct answers.

(A) Black holes have strong gravitational pulls that even light cannot escape.

(B) Planets have their own light sources.

(C) Moons always have an atmosphere.

(D) Nebulas are clouds of gas and dust in space.

(E) Comets remain stationary in space.

32. Which of the following describes the primary reason for the difference in temperature between day and night on Earth?

(A) The Earth's rotation on its axis.

(B) The Earth's revolution around the Sun.

(C) The Sun moving closer to and farther from Earth.

(D) The moon blocking the Sun's light at night.

33. Which statements correctly describe the characteristics of Earth and the moon? Select TWO correct answers.

(A) Earth has a breathable atmosphere, while the moon does not.

(B) The moon produces its own light, while Earth does not.

(C) Earth has liquid water, while the moon does not.

(D) The moon is larger than Earth.

(E) Earth and the moon have the same gravity.

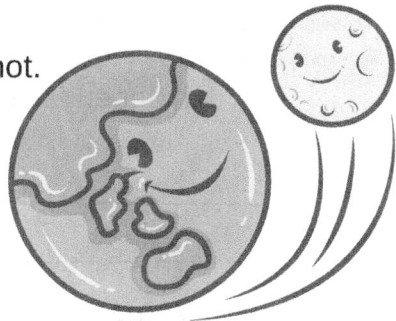

34. Why do we have a leap year every four years?

A) Because the Earth's orbit around the Sun takes 365.25 days.

B) Because the moon's orbit around Earth affects our calendar.

C) Because the Sun's energy output changes every four years.

D) Because of changes in Earth's axial tilt.

35. What is the largest land animal on Earth?

A) Blue Whale

B) African Elephant

C) Giraffe

D) Hippopotamus

36. The Plant Growth Experiment:

Sarah and Jack are experimenting with different amounts of sunlight on plant growth.

Sarah places one plant in a sunny window and another plant in a dark cupboard. What do you think will happen to each plant over time?

A) The plant in the sunny window will grow taller because it receives more sunlight for photosynthesis.

B) The plant in the dark cupboard will grow taller because it conserves energy without sunlight.

C) Both plants will grow at the same rate because they are the same type of plant.

D) It depends on the type of plants Sarah is growing.

_____

_____

_____

92 _____

_____

37. A group of animals is shown.

Tiger   Monkey   Snake

Which habitat are these animals BEST suited for?

A) A dense rainforest with tall trees and thick underbrush.

B) A polar ice cap with frozen seas and little vegetation.

C) A hot desert with sand dunes and cacti.

D) A shallow estuary with brackish water and tidal movements.

38. A student is pushing a shopping cart across a parking lot. What change will reduce the amount of force needed to move the shopping cart?

A) Increase the weight of the items in the cart.

B) Decrease the size of the wheels on the cart.

C) Push the cart on a rougher surface.

D) Push the cart with a longer handle.

39. What type of energy is stored in a stretched rubber band?

A) Kinetic energy

B) Thermal energy

C) Potential energy

D) Mechanical energy

40. Which force keeps planets in orbit around the Sun?

(A) Friction

(B) Gravity

(C) Tension

(D) Air resistance

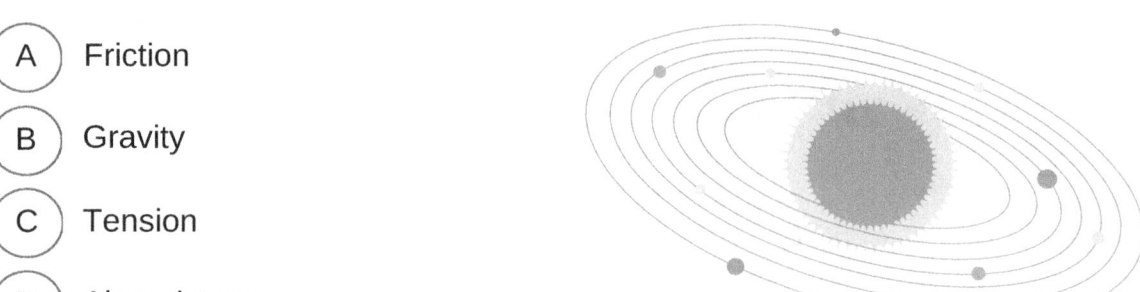

41. Students want to investigate how the angle of a ramp affects the speed of a toy car rolling down on it. Which procedure should they follow for their experiment?

(A) Measure the speed of the toy car rolling down ramps of different angles. Conduct three trials for each angle.

(B) Measure the speed of the toy car rolling down the same ramp at different times of the day. Conduct three trials for each time.

(C) Measure the speed of the toy car rolling down ramps of different angles using different toy cars. Conduct three trials for each car.

(D) Measure the speed of the toy car rolling down the same ramp at the same angle using different students. Conduct three trials for each student.

42. The circuit has five lightbulbs and four switches. If Switch 1 and 2 are closed which lightbulbs will glow? Write the answer on the line provided. If none of the lightbulbs will glow, write NONE on the line: _____

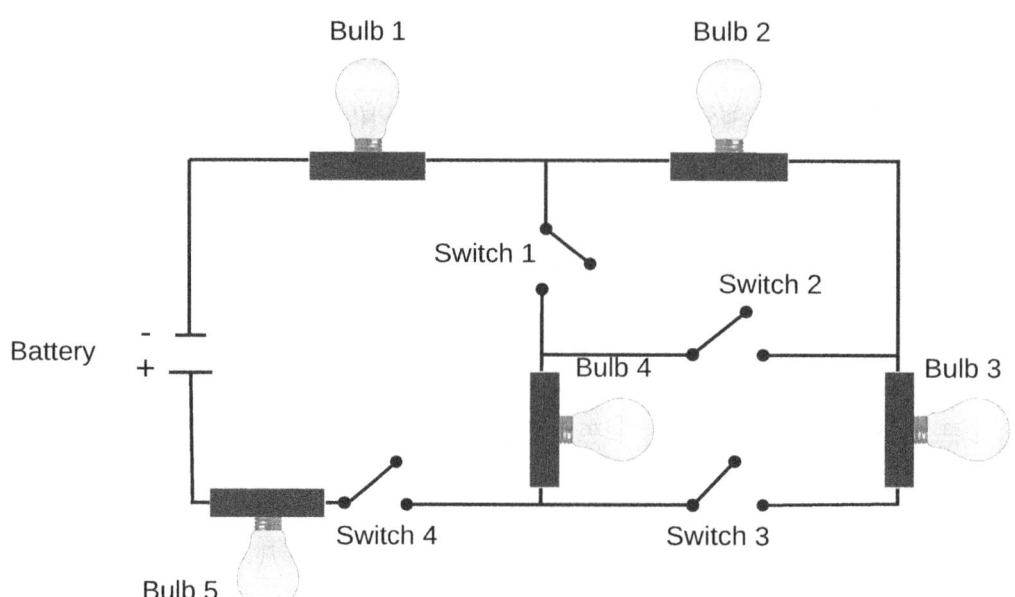

43. This question has two parts. First, answer Part A. Then, based on your answer to Part A, answer Part B.

Part A
A student studies two planets: Mars and Jupiter. Which statement BEST describes a key difference between Mars and Jupiter?

(A) Jupiter is a rocky planet with a thin atmosphere, while Mars is a gas giant with thick clouds of hydrogen and helium.

(B) Mars has rings made of ice and rock particles, while Jupiter has no visible rings around its equator.

(C) Mars orbits closer to the Sun and has a reddish appearance due to iron oxide on its surface, while Jupiter orbits farther away and appears as a bright, striped gas giant.

(D) Mars has a solid surface covered with water oceans, while Jupiter has a turbulent surface with active volcanoes.

Part B
Based on your answer to Part A, which statement BEST explains how this difference in appearance or orbit helps each planet?

(A) Mars' closer orbit to the Sun results in higher temperatures, which help maintain its iron-rich surface coloration.

(B) Mars's position farther from the Sun allows for a colder environment, which promotes the formation of its extensive cloud layers.

(C) Mars' reddish appearance makes it less visible to telescopes compared to Jupiter's bright clouds, which aids in studying its surface features.

(D) Jupiter's striped appearance is caused by the planet's rapid rotation and strong magnetic field, which create distinct atmospheric bands.

44. What happens to the particles in a substance when it is heated?

(A) They move slower and get closer together.

(B) They move faster and spread apart.

(C) They stop moving completely.

(D) They change shape.

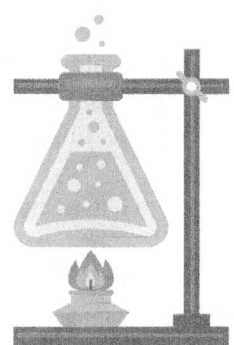

Answers Practice Test 5

1. A. Saturn
2. B. The Sun
3. D. Pacific Ocean
4. A. Lichens → caribou → wolves → polar bears
5. C. Leads to loss of habitat, reduces biodiversity, and contributes to climate change.
6. B. Bacteria
7. C. Carbon dioxide
8. A. Metamorphosis
9. D. Thermal energy from the stove burner.
10. A. The smoke particles reflect the laser light.
11. B. Gravity pulling the book downward.
12. C. Water has a similar density to the particles'.
13. B. Balloon B, because it has more air.
Explanation: In physics, the motion of an object propelled by air (like a balloon) depends on the amount of air (mass) and the force exerted (thrust). Balloon B, being larger and filled with more air, experiences a greater force of propulsion when released, resulting in faster movement across the room compared to Balloon A, which has less air and therefore less force. This scenario introduces the concept of thrust and mass affecting the motion of objects propelled by air in a fun and interactive context.
14. B. By breaking up dirt and grease into smaller pieces.
15. A. Dissolve the mixture in water and then filter it.
16. A. Substance A, because it is softer.
Explanation: In chemistry, the melting point of a substance refers to the temperature at which it changes from a solid to a liquid state. Generally, substances with lower melting points will melt faster at room temperature compared to substances with higher melting points. Butter (Substance A) typically has a lower melting point than chocolate (Substance B) due to its composition of fats and water content.
Therefore, Butter (Substance A) is expected to melt faster when exposed to the same environmental conditions.
17. D. Sample 5 is oxygen.
18. A. Lizard
19. B. Both are created by glacial erosion.
20. A. Jupiter is closer to the sun than Saturn.
21. D. The dye was absorbed into the fabric's fibers.
22. B. Desert
23. A. The Earth tilts away from the Sun, resulting in less direct sunlight.
24. B. Shallow ponds with muddy bottoms.
25. B. Metamorphic rocks

26. C. They conduct heat well.
27. B. Reduced habitats for wetland species.
28. C. To reach high leaves.
29. C. Plastic toy
30. B. Both will fall at the same rate.
31. A. Black holes have strong gravitational pulls that even light cannot escape.
  D. Nebulas are clouds of gas and dust in space.
32. A. The Earth's rotation on its axis.
33. A. Earth has a breathable atmosphere, while the moon does not.
 C. Earth has liquid water, while the moon does not.
34. A. Because the Earth's orbit around the sun takes 365.25 days.
35. B. African Elephant
36. A. The plant in the sunny window will grow taller because it receives more sunlight for photosynthesis.
Explanation: In biology, sunlight is crucial for photosynthesis, the process by which plants convert light energy into chemical energy (glucose) to fuel their growth and development. Plants placed in sunny locations receive more energy from sunlight, allowing them to produce more glucose and grow taller compared to plants in low-light conditions.
37. A. A dense rainforest with tall trees and thick underbrush.
38. D. Push the cart with a longer handle.
39. C. Potential energy
40. B. Gravity
41. A. Measure the speed of the toy car rolling down ramps of different angles. Conduct three trials for each angle.
42. NONE
43. C. Mars orbits closer to the Sun and has a reddish appearance due to iron oxide on its surface, while Jupiter orbits farther away and appears as a bright, striped gas giant.
  A. Mars' closer orbit to the Sun results in higher temperatures, which help maintain its iron-rich surface coloration.
44. B. They move faster and spread apart.

Made in the USA
Coppell, TX
30 May 2025